CHRISTIAN LIVING SERIES

~ Volume 3 ~

Christian Living Series

~ Volume 3 ~

Christian VIRTUES

by His Grace Bishop Youanis

ST SHENOUDA'S MONASTERY
SYDNEY, AUSTRALIA
2013

Christian Living Series - Volume 3
CHRISTIAN VIRTUES

ST SHENOUDA MONASTERY
8419 Putty Rd,
Putty, NSW, 2330
Sydney, Australia

www.stshenoudamonastery.org.au

ISBN 13: 978-0-9873400-3-0

All scripture quotations, unless otherwise indicated, are taken from the New King James Version®. Copyright © 1982 by Thomas Nelson, Inc. Used by permission. All rights reserved.

Cover Design:
Hani Ghaly,
Begoury Graphics
begourygraphics@gmail.com

Contents

Purity   7

Prayer   51

Fasting   129

Almsgiving   165

Purity

𝒏

"He who overcomes his body, has overcome his nature and rises above it. He who is above human nature shares the angelic nature."
(St. John of the Ladder)

❧ The Honour of Purity

❧ Youth and Purity

❧ Fights of Youth's Sinful Desires

❧ How to Acquire Purity

❧ Spiritual Guards

❧ Remedy

❧ After the Fall

❧ Dreams and Wet Dreams

❧ Important Guidelines

THE HONOUR OF PURITY

St Paul says, "For this is the will of God, your sanctification: that you should abstain from sexual immorality... For God did not call us to uncleanness, but to holiness." (1 Thes. 4: 3,7) Holiness refers to chastity and purity, both of which contradict adultery and impurity. "For I am jealous for you with godly jealousy. For I have betrothed you to one husband that I may present you as a chaste virgin to Christ." (2 Cor.11: 2)

It is the life of angels in heaven as mentioned by the Lord Jesus, "For in the resurrection they neither marry nor are given in marriage, but are like angels of God in heaven. "(Matt. 22: 30) St Cyprian addressed some virgins assuring the same; "Now while living on earth, you are starting to enjoy life in heaven after resurrection. By preserving your virginity, you are resembling the angels."

St. John Cassian also says: "There is no other virtue equal to chastity because when one lives in chastity while in the body, he controls his troublesome body and lives in the Spirit, as mentioned, "But you are not in the flesh but in the Spirit, if indeed the Spirit of God dwells in you. Now if anyone does not have the Spirit of Christ, he is not His." (Rom. 8: 9) The human beings who live in chastity and purity are more sublime than the angels who do not have bodies battling against the spirit."

God honours this virtue. When He wanted to send His Only Begotten Son, born of a woman, He chose a pure

Virgin living a life of chastity and purity. Saints Ironimus and Augustine say; "Lord Jesus used to love St. John the discicple more than the others because of his celibacy. Solomon says, "He who loves purity of heart, and has grace on his lips, the king will be his friend." (Prov. 22: 11) Many interpreters say that it befits St John the celibate who used to lean on Jesus' chest. Although the other disciples couldn't ask Jesus for this favour, John did (John 21: 20). When Lord Jesus appeared on Tiberias Sea after His Holy Resurrection, no one knew Him except John (John 21: 107). St Ironimus commented on this incident saying; "No one knew Him except John the celibate, because the celibate recognised Jesus the celibate, the Son of the Virgin."

In the Book of Revelation, John announced the honour of chastity and purity in heaven, when he talked about the 144,000 virgins, "Then I looked, and behold, a Lamb standing on Mount Zion, and with Him one hundred and forty-four thousand, having His Father's name written on their foreheads. And I heard a voice from heaven, like the voice of many waters, and like the voice of loud thunder. And I heard the sound of harpists playing their harps. They sang as it were a new song before the throne, before the four living creatures, and the elders; and no one could learn that song except the hundred and forty-four thousand who were redeemed from the earth. These are the ones who were not defiled with women, for they are virgins. These are the ones who follow the Lamb wherever He goes. These were redeemed from among men, being firstfruits to God and to the Lamb. And in their mouth was found no deceit, for they are without fault before the throne of God." (Rev. 14: 1-4) The 144 000 virgins were the only ones singing a special hymn and following the Lamb wherever He went; a proof of the sublime life of purity and chastity.

On the contrary, adultery and impurity are highly rejected by God. As punishment, God destroyed the entire world through the flood, burnt Sodom and Gomorrah and killed 23,000 Israelites in one day after adultery occurred with the daughters of Moab. As a result of adultery, David was disadvantaged and his Son, Solomon bowed to idols. In general, God's wrath was against His people because, "They do not direct their deeds toward turning to their God, for the spirit of harlotry is in their midst, and they do not know the Lord." (Hosea 5: 4) For this reason, St Paul the Apostle warns us saying, "For this you know, that no fornicator, unclean person, nor covetous man, who is an idolater, has any inheritance in the kingdom of Christ and God. Let no one deceive you with empty words, for because of these things the wrath of God comes upon the sons of disobedience." (Eph. 5: 5-6)

The power of the Lord is removed from the person who is enslaved by this sin. When Noah sent the pigeon, it came back because it couldn't find rest amongst dead corpses. It is the same with the Spirit of the Lord. Similar to this pigeon, it can never dwell in impure bodies, but only in pure ones.

YOUTH AND THE LIFE OF PURITY

Without a doubt, sexual issues are the biggest obstacles which prevent youth from living a life of purity. Some might think that it is impossible for a youth to live in purity, but this is not true. We have so many examples in the Holy Bible and church history refuting this belief.

Man was created pure in the image of God. Since God wants Man to be pure, He gave him all the capabilities to live pure and remain pure. So how can we doubt the support given by God?

If we study the sins of youth, we will discover that the individual himself is the one who runs towards the sin. St Philoxinious says: "Desire overcomes us, not because it is stronger, but because we are reluctant. It can never fight you, unless you willingly allow the fight to start."

THE SECRET OF A POWERFUL YOUTH

The power of a youth lies in his chastity and purity. The person who controls his sexual life, controls every aspect in his life. However, he who cannot control his desires, is a failure in his entire life. This is proved by examples from the Holy Bible, church history and even daily life experiences:

Samson the Mighty; who killed hundreds of Philistines, was humiliated when he yielded to his desires, "And it came to pass, when she pestered him daily with her words and pressed him, so that his soul was vexed to death, that he told her all his heart….Then she lulled him to sleep on her knees, and called for a man and had him shave off the seven locks of his head. Then she began to torment him and his strength left him…Then the Philistines took him and put out his eyes, and brought him down to Gaza. They bound him with bronze fetters, and he became a grinder in the prison." (Judges 16). On the other hand, Joseph the Righteous; was living in purity and was honest to his God and to Potiphar his master; thus the Lord delivered him from prison and made him an overseer to the Egyptians and to neighbouring countries. (Gen. 41)

Pope Metthaous, the 87th was a shepherd. One day, the devil tried to make him fall into the sin of impurity. A lady came and started talking to him while shephering his flock. When he asked her about the reason of her admiration, she answered; "It is your beautiful eyebrows". Immediately he scraped his eyebrows and went back to the lady saying, "Here, take the hair of my eyebrows which you desired." The lady got terrified yet was amazed at his boldness and his strong hold of purity.

A STORY

A pure virgin was living in peace while a youth started coming to her house and annoying her, claiming that he admired her. It happened that one day she asked him, "What do you admire the most." He answered, "Your eyes my young lady, so beautiful, they infuriate my heart with love when I look at them". The girl was sewing, so she took the needle and plucked out one of her eyes and threw it to him. When she was about to do the same with the other eye, the youth stopped her and was so sorry for what she did. He left her and headed straight to the wilderness where he became a monk.

A SECOND STORY

During the invasion of the Arab to Jerusalem, the soldiers attacked a convent and took a beautiful nun, offering her as a present to the leader of their legion. When he tried to spoil her purity, she said; "Wait a bit, my master, I've learnt something from other nuns. I have a magic oil, if placed on someone's neck, a sword or any other weapon could never cut this neck. Definitely you need to use it because you are a soldier and you fight a lot". He then asked, "How can I make sure that you are telling the truth about this oil?" She answered, "Here is the oil, put some on your neck and let me try to cut your head with your sword." He answered, "No, you try it first and I will try to cut off your head." Happily, she gave him the oil and stretched her neck ready for the sword. When he hit her neck with all his might, her head rolled down on the floor and blood was all over the place. This leader wept bitterly for killing such a beautiful girl. He then discovered that she had tricked him and preferred to die rather than to defile her virginity and fall in sin and impurity.

A THIRD STORY

During the era of Roman persecution against the Christians in Egypt, the Roman rulers were greatly astonished because of the firm steadfastness of the Christians' faith. The rulers were shocked as the Christians preferred to die than to deny their faith. Finally they comprehended the secret of this strong faith, which was their desire for purity and chastity. Consequently, the rulers started to use different methods to spoil their purity.

A youth refused to deny his faith so they tied him to a bed and got a woman who lied next to him, trying to arouse his desire. When he couldn't find a way to escape, he cut his tongue with his teeth and threw it in her face, full of blood. The woman was frightened, kept screaming and quickly ran and left him.

A FOURTH STORY

St. Theodora and St. Didimus were martyrs during the era of Diolectian. The governor, after failing to spoil St. Theodora's purity, placed her in a brothel. However, a Christian youth called Didimus was able to trick the guards of this brothel and set her free by changing clothes with her and staying there. When the trick was discovered, the governor ordered to cut off his head and throw his body in the fire. While the soldiers were taking him to fulfil the order, they saw Theodora running after him, saying in reproach, "My brother, why are you stealing my crown?" The solders arrested her and they both won the crown of martyrdom in the year 302 A.D.

These are just a few examples of the heroes of purity, as they faced mighty governors and rulers courageously, only because they knew how to control their desires. Solomon the Wise says, "He who is slow to anger is better than the mighty, and he who rules his spirit than he who takes a city." (Prov. 16: 32)

Fights of Youths' Sinful Desires

St Philoxinous says, "Preserve yourself from the things which attract you to lust, block all the entries, thus you are shielding yourself. Desire might start from the body or from the mind, or from external sources, thus, we have to discern the reasons and block them wherever they are coming from." This saint summarized three reasons that attract us to sinful desires:

The Body

Referring to the energy of the body, relaxation or illness.

1. The heat of the body is a result of adolscent stage and youth. Excessive foods also result in excessive energy, especially eating specific kinds such as chilli which causes commotion. Certain drinks exhaust the nerves.

2. Relaxation of the body is a result of laziness, resting more than needed and taking too much sleep.

3. The illness of the body is any disorder in the glands which causes sexual rampage. This needs medical assistance. Body illness can also refer to the sensitivity of the sexual system as a result of practicing sin for a long time. Consequently, the body becomes very sensitive and is affected by any reason.

THE THOUGHTS

Referring to defiled thoughts which haunt a person and press the mind constantly.

This could be the result of an empty mind, i.e. nothing useful is occupying the mind. Sometimes this is a devilish war against pure saints. The devil uses it to defile the mind with lustful desires.

EXTERNAL REASONS

These are the stumbling blocks which come to us through our senses. The senses are the gates of information and the gates of stumble for a person. The eye sees exciting sights and the ear hears bad words. In both cases, sight and hearing are connected to the thought, and from here comes the sin.

1. The Sight:

The sight is a vital gate to youthful sins. Consequently, St Augustine considered it the first step of falling. This could be through looking lustfully at the other gender or looking through bad magazines, movies, television or reading obscene books that deal with sexual issues in the wrong manner.

2. Hearing:

This sense opens up your mind to dirty jokes and conversations from bad friends. Consequently, arousing bad thoughts and sexual desires.

3. Touch:

We can recognise the danger of this sense in an overcrowded place. It is also the direct reason for masturbation. Generally speaking, our presence at any place of sin will quickly reduce our spiritual resistance. If a piece of iron comes in contact with a magnetic orbit, it will get attracted and acquire the characteristics of the original magnet. There is no way the piece of iron can go back to its origin unless it escapes away from the magnetic orbit. Similarly, if we put ourselves in a bad orbit, as weak human beings, we will get attracted to it. We will not be able to return to our original purity unless we abandon this sinful atmosphere.

A Spiritual Elder says; "This is the order of the children of God's senses: Prevent your eyes from looking at human beauty, instead, look at God. Prevent your ears from hearing obscene words, instead, listen to the secrets of the Mighty. Beware of smelling bad aromas, and close your mouth in total awareness because this leads to total destruction. Preserve your tongue from void conversations as it is sufficient for you to talk to God, Your Creator. Finally, handle the fifth sense; which is touch; to the Vigilant Protector, ask for purity in all your movements so that the Lord might protect you from unclean thoughts".

OTHER REASONS

1. Most Dangerous Case:

The most dangerous case is when sexual feelings becomes a permanent desire inside the heart. The mind gets occupied with sexual pictures, imagines sexual situations and lives with that feeling all the time. Finally, he loses his simplicity and expects defilement in everything, even innocent incidents. The whole body becomes aroused and the mind is full of sexual thoughts and emotions.

Lord Jesus says, "But I say to you that whoever looks at a woman to lust for her has already committed adultery with her in his heart." (Matt. 5: 28) He didn't say, " whoever looks at a woman has already committed adultery with her." Therefore, the main issue in this sin is the desire; "Then, when desire has conceived, it gives birth to sin; and sin, when it is full-grown, brings forth death." (James 1: 15). There is great cooperation between the four sources of desire, whether through the heart, thought, senses or body. Wherever desire starts, it defiles the rest of the sources and so on.

The horrible fact about sexual sin, is that it consumes everything in a human being; his body, soul, mind and senses. Moreover, when someone sins sexually, his fall is a huge one and everything is destroyed within him. St Paul says, "Flee sexual immorality. Every sin that a man does is outside the body, but he who commits sexual immorality sins against his own body." (1 Cor. 6: 18)

2. Pride:

Someone might ask: What is the relationship between pride and adultery?

The answer is very clear: The Heavenly grace departs a proud person because of his pride. As a result, he falls in sin and the Lord allows this to happen so that he might feel weak and humiliated, thus regret his pride and humble himself. There is no greater sin which humiliates a spiritually proud person more than falling into adultery. Adultery is sometimes referred to as the sin of impurity because of its awfulness. St John of the Ladder says, "If you do not get rid of pride, you can never conquer adultery or any other sin." He also says, "No one ever conquered his body except he who humbled his heart, and no one ever humbled his heart except he who killed his desires." The early saintly fathers say: "The person who is proud of his asceticism falls into adultery, and he who is proud of being knowledgeable falls into blasphemy."

Adultery hides in pride while judgment protects it. Do not allow yourself to condemn or mock a person who falls into sexual sins, but have mercy and pray for him that the Lord might lift him up, and that his fall might be a reason for his humility. Always remember that you are a weak human being, at a risk of experiencing pains and temptations exactly like him. Tell yourself "He had fallen today, I might fall tomorrow." If you are a person who rushes into condemning and despising others, be sure that one day, God will teach you an unforgettable lesson, that is to discover your weakness. Maybe God will allow you to fall into the same sin. St Paul says, "Do not be haughty, but fear." (Rom. 11: 20)

Examine yourself, my dear; examine your spiritual path. Maybe your sexual desires are a result of your pride which caused the Divine grace to abandon you.

There are two vital issues related to sexuality: love and energy. Each person has the emotion of love. If this emotion is not directed properly, the devil can use it in sexual lust and desires. However, those who have satisfied this emotion correctly and spiritually are very comfortable when it comes to sexual issues. Some examples of satisfying the emotion of love in a proper manner:

1. Visiting the sick: Love here is shown in a caring sympathetic manner. It is very hard to get sexual fights while performing such a love.

2. Visiting the poor, widows and orphans: This may be in orphanages or other locations of social services.

3. Different spiritual services: such as calming those in hardships, comforting the grieving or visiting prisoners.

4. Tutoring: Such as serving in Sunday school classes and experiencing all the lovely feelings related to this service; parenting, care, love and friendship.

5. Friendships: An isolated person, who has no friends to exchange love and friendship, could easily fall into sexual fights, to make up for the lack of love inside his heart. So if you want to escape these fights, have good relationships with faithful friends and protect yourself from sin.

6. Patriotic love and hobbies: Such as getting engaged in patriotic activities, writing poetry, playing music and all sorts of useful hobbies.

Each one has a certain level of energy and enthusiasm, and if it is not used in a useful way, one will certainly slip into harmful sexual desires. So a person, who uses his energy in playing sports or social service, will not face as much fights as a person who lives in relaxation and excessive bodily rest.

DIFFERENT STAGES OF SIN

Sexual issues go through different stages, depending on how severe or deep they are. Every stage needs an appropriate remedy. On the other hand, there are general tips which befit any of the following stages:

1. A fight from outside, while the heart is pure from inside.

2. A superficial response to sin, not thinking too much about it.

3. A severe indulgence through the mind, heart and senses. This is divided into two parts: one part is where sin is present and a person is ready to commit it. The second part is where sin is far and the person is trying hard to commit it.

4. The fourth stage is when sin becomes a habit.

HOW TO ACQUIRE PURITY

PROTECTIVE METHODS

1. Staying away from the sources of sin:

You know where sin comes from, so try to block these gates. Stay away from all powerful sources whether seeing, listening, touching, reading, meetings, places or anything that brings impure memories.

You have to know that human beings could be affected by good or evil. Don't ever believe that you are strong and capable of resisting, because you are not stronger than David the Prophet, about whom God said, "I have found David, the son of Jesse, a man after My own heart, who will do all My will." (Acts 13: 22) Although this, he couldn't resist one scene and he fell into sin. (2 Sam. 11) You are not stronger than Samson the Mighty who, although he knew what Delilah was after, couldn't hold his secret, revealed his vow, and finally lost his honour and dignity. You are not stronger than Solomon, the wisest person of his age, whose wives diverted his heart and made him far from God. Regarding this sin, Solomon specifically said, "For she has cast down many wounded, and all who were slain by her were strong men." (Prov.7: 26)

Don't think that escaping from sin is a coward or weak attitude. It is the initial and main remedy for this defiled war. Remember that Joseph the Righteous, the representative of chastity and purity, fled from Potiphar's wife. This made him a hero and no one ever said that his flee was a coward act.

Joshua Son of Sirach says, "Never trust your enemy, for as a brass pot, his wickedness rusts." (Sirach 12: 10) Never trust your body. As iron can rust, the body can produce evil desires. Even if your body is calm, it can commit sin in a twinkle of an eye. Your body may have never attacked in years, but it can in any moment.

St. John of the Ladder says, "A cunning fox pretends to be sleeping or dead in order to attack its prey. Then it jumps, kills and devours. This is the same with the devil of adultery; it calms down the body for a while, deceiving the soul, then it attacks. Never trust your body until you meet Lord Christ".

Solomon the Wise said about the sin of impurity, "Can a man take fire to his bosom, and his clothes not be burned? Can one walk on hot coals, and his feet not be seared?" (Prov. 6: 27, 28) Even though you may have won an attack and didn't actually fall into sin, you may have got stains on the way, or have stored bad memories and experiences, which might attack you at a period of weakness!

If you enter a flour mill, even without touching anything, some fine white particles of flour will cover your clothes. If a person wearing white clothes fights with a miner, the lovely white costume will have some coal dust staining it! If a person wearing white fights a man with muddy hands, the white clothes will also have muddy stains on them. The same case applies with youthful lusts and excitements. It will leave some prints in our lives. Solomon the Wise says, "A wise man fears and departs from evil, but a fool rages and is self-confident." (Prov. 14:

16) This means that a person who fears and avoids sin is a wise man, while he who trusts in himself is a fool.

Those who come in contact with sin, even if it doesn't affect them directly and immediately, it can work and affect them slowly, then suddenly attack. A strong will which doesn't fall immediately, might get weaker gradually, "Escape for your life! Do not look behind you nor stay anywhere in the plain." (Gen. 19: 17). By escaping excitements and stumbles, we mean a continuous escape. Many started a life of purity and humility, but when they felt their strength and victory, they started to loosen their restrictions. As a result, sin crept into their lives and stole away all their previous resistance.

Some people fall into sin by guiding and directing others out. This situation starts with a person listening to the sexual problems and temptations of others; he might even do some research in attempt to help others. As a result, his mind gets filled with sinful thoughts and he remembers his own memories. We advice those people to refrain from carrying this mission, especially if they are not spiritually prepared. Always be honest with yourself.

2. Fill Your Leisure Time:

Leisure time is beneficial for a person who is advanced spiritually and who is successful in his prayers, meditations and recitations. However, for a person facing sexual fights, leisure time is a fatal enemy. He should stay apart from it. If you want to protect yourself from entering into a sexual war, lest you should fall, try to avoid leisure time. Keep yourself occupied at all times, so that when the devil of desire tries to attract you, he finds you busy with other useful matters. Doing this, you have benefited from getting rid of sexual fights and all the impurity and pain related to it. Furthermore, you are advantaged in that you occupy your time with good deeds. These good deeds might include:

<u>a) Sincerity in your studies or job:</u>

A student who studies hard is busy with his books and research; hence he is preparing himself for a bright future and gaining trust and respect from his teachers, family and friends. In addition, he is protecting himself from sexual wars. We always notice that students are less likely to fall into sexual sins during the period of exams, than other periods of the year. The benefits of being sincere in your job also apply.

<u>b) Reading:</u>

A person who reads a lot becomes knowledgeable and keeps his mind busy with different subjects. We don't mean only spiritual readings, but also general knowledge. The brain gets occupied and thinks about what is being read. Reading enlightens the brain. St Anthony says, "Read a lot, for reading rids you from all impurity." St. Isaac says, "Repeat what you've read from the spiritual books and biographies of saints. The more you read and meditate, the more you are filled with holy thoughts, and can easily practice the fear of God and belittle hardships."

We recommend deeper readings if you feel sin is approaching you. Sexual thoughts could still attack you if your readings are not deep and precious. Concentrate and think about what you are reading so that you are totally occupied and leave no room for any impure thoughts. The best type of readings are those that need us to think of a solution to a special situation. Similarly, an interesting story that you yearn to finish, or an important issue which adds to the mental treasure.

Styles and preferences of readings might differ from one person to another; whether the subject is a spiritual, social or moral one. It also depends on your age and intellectual and spiritual level. Reading spiritual books on Christianity requires deep concentration and thinking. For example books dealing with denominational differences. Also, various intellectual books, such as science, require concentration and thinking. It also raises the holy zeal, which means the mind and the heart are fully occupied, and there is no room for any sexual fights. We recommend reading based on an arranged schedule or spiritual practice.

c) Social Activities:

Reading might not be suitable for some people or would be of little benefit. Thus, you can occupy yourself with social activities, such as serving the poor, needy, sick, orphans and widows. Furthermore, comforting the grieving, supporting those in tribulations, serving in remote villages, Sunday school classes and so on.

d) Hobbies:

You can fill your leisure time with different hobbies according to your interest; drawing, photography, handicraft, and many others. In addition, writing poetry, playing music and church tunes. For example, a person who is learning church tunes, might spend a lot of time practicing and revising. It also gives them a chance to actively participate with others in general worship and during the Holy Liturgy. It opens a door for spending some time with church friends. All of these practices keep us busy, refraining us from defiled sexual thoughts.

e) Sports:

St. Paul the Apostle says, "...for bodily exercise profits a little." (2 Tim. 4: 8) There is no doubt, some of the 'little' are facing sexual fights. Some people might not like reading or any personal hobbies, but they may enjoy physical exercise and sports. This is fine, but we advise them to choose a sport with pure faithful friends, to establish a healthy atmosphere. Sports Clubs organised in spiritual organisations are great, especially if supervised by spiritual leaders.

3. Positive Protection:

Positive protection from sexual sin is not only the love of chastity, but it also includes general progress and development in the spiritual life. A person who progresses spiritually and hates sin, will grow in the love of Lord Jesus Christ and will feel the triviality of this vain world. Consequently, he will refrain from sexual sin exactly like any other bodily desire. On the other hand, a person who loves the world and its lustful desires, will certainly yield to sexual sins, as a continuation of the bodily desires he is enjoying.

As a means of protection from sexual sins, try to practice the life of the spiritual sublime, expressed by St John when he says, "Do not love the world or the things in the world." (1 John 2: 15) This is very true; for the youth who comes regularly to church and practices all its rituals, will definitely reach this level of resisting sexual sins. The more they love God, get closer to Him, and look forward to enjoy eternal life with Him, the more they renounce the desires of the world. Their sexual desires become sublime and their stored energy as youth is dealt with in a proper physical and spiritual manner.

SPIRITUAL GUARDS

GUIDELINES TO HELP IN THIS SPIRITUAL COURSE:

1. Fasting:

When it comes to fasting, it has to be practiced in its ideal way; resisting the desires of the body, abstaining from kinds of food craved for, and abstaining till a certain hour of the day. This will lead to strengthening your will and controlling other body desires, including sexual issues. As for those who fast and feel successful, yet they fail in sexual desires, we advise them to examine themselves deeply in their practices of fasting. St John of the Ladder says, "He who is fighting adultery but doesn't control his eating habits resembles a person who quenches the fire with oil and hay. Also he who is fighting adultery with fasting only without humbling himself, resembles a person swimming in the great ocean using one hand."

2. Prayers:

Practicing prayers gives you a kind of shyness as you cannot stand before God to pray and indulge in sexual thoughts. We advise you to increase your prayers so that you might increase your holy shyness, and your mind becomes more enlightened with the Lord. Prayers also give you a special help against sexual fights.

Through prayers, you remind yourself of the covenant you have with the Lord, that is, to lead a holy life. Every time you fall into sexual sin, you are breaching this covenant. Some people refrain from sin after prayers, and so, gradually, they totally conquer. However, beware, because the devil might leave you for a while, then start war again. Don't wait until you are living in entire purity then pray, but pray in order to reach purity. Always know that being shy is a useful thing, because it makes you think deeply about your relationship with God, encouraging you to resist sin and so on.

Occupy your mind with meditations and repeat divine sayings. Recite Psalms, Praises and Hymns. Concerning this issue St Isaac says: "Talking a lot about virtue, renews the desire for virtue at all times." Also, "As a big pot brings forth flame and fire, repeating holy practices will bring forth warmth and holy zeal."

3. Meditate on the Lord's Sufferings:

Meditating constantly on our Lord Jesus Christ's pains and sufferings for our salvation will increase our shyness and submission. Reproach yourself and think: How can you enjoy these lustful desires, while Jesus on the Cross, is wounded because of your iniquities and transgressions?

Remember Uriah's words, "And Uriah said to David, "The ark and Israel and Judah are dwelling in tents, and my lord Joab and the servants of my lord are encamped in the open fields. Shall I then go to my house to eat and drink, and to lie with my wife? As you live, and as your soul lives, I will not do this thing." (2Sam.11: 11)

St. Augustine says: "The best remedy for fighting adulterous thoughts is by meditating on the sufferings and Death of my Master Lord Jesus Christ."

4. Confession:

Practice confession properly and honestly. Never be ashamed to disclose your thoughts to your confession father because then, you will gain great Divine support. Firstly, the devil of adultery steps backwards as soon as he is exposed. Secondly, the guidance, directions and prayers of your confession father will support you. Thirdly, as you confess your weaknesses, your humility before the Lord will be rewarded. All of the reasons mentioned above will pour heavenly support and will help you to progress in the path of virtue.

5. Partaking of Holy Communion:

After confession, you will benefit a lot from partaking of Holy Communion. Holy Communion gives a great power and strength in fighting sexual desire. St Makarious the Great says: "Holy Communion protects you from the enemies. He, who is reluctant with this Mystery, gives a chance to the power of darkness to overcome him." St John Chrysostom also says: "After partaking of the Holy Communion, let's consider ourselves like lions blazing with the fire of love, and then the devils will get terrified of us."

6. Biography of Saints:

Reading the biography of saints is very beneficial for the life of purity, because it puts a role model before our eyes. We also get affected and attracted to follow in their steps; thus, spontaneously we refrain from sexual desires. Reading sexual books stimulate a person's emotions. On the contrary, reading about the saints stimulates a love for purity and virtue. St. Isaac says: "The news of the saints is very desirable in the ears of the meek, like water to new plants. Always think of God's providence with the elderly fathers, as good ointment to the eye. Remember the saints at all times; repeat their sayings and thoughts so that you might resemble them."

7. Ascetic Books:

Reading ascetic books and spiritual books generally directs the feelings and desires of a person towards heavenly matters. It also makes him hate sin and look for his salvation. You will gain more benefit if these readings are accompanied with spiritual practices.

8. Books about Eternity and Judgment:

Reading books which deal with Judgment Day and eternity will stimulate the fear of God and lead to the love of God, as mentioned, "The fear of God is the beginning of wisdom." (Ps.111: 10) St Augustine says: "Fear prepares room for love, thus, if there is no fear, love can never dwell in your heart." St Anthony also says, "The fear of God is the beginning of wisdom. When a house is lit, darkness disappears. It is same with the fear of God. When fear enters someone's heart, it dismisses ignorance and teaches virtues and wisdom."

My dear brethren, that's why we recommend you to read a lot about death, judgment, eternal life and punishment. Read about the soul and its fate while waiting for Judgment Day. Read the Book of Revelation and the fathers' interpretation. Attend funerals and go to graves. Console the families of the departed ones. Finally, sit and think about your own fate and perform works that befit repentance.

9. Reading biographies of pure saints:

It is of great help when you read lives of pure and chaste saints, who resisted sin in amazing persistence and assertion. They never allowed themselves to find excuses to yield or submit to sin. Instead, they obeyed God till death and "...resisted to bloodshed, striving against sin." (Heb. 12: 4)

Another high level of spirituality includes those saints whose families forced them to get married, yet they lived in celibacy till they departed in peace. For example, St Makarious the Great, St Amoun, St John Kama, Pope Demetrius the Vinedresser and many others. Others were forced by their masters. For example, St Malkhos whose biography was penned by St. Ironimus. Also, St Samuel the Confessor who was captured by the Barbarians, then tied for years to look after the camels with another female slave.

10. Reading Repentance Stories:

It is very beneficial to read stories of repentant saints and how they repented after living in sin for years. Examples include: St. Maria the niece of St. Ibrahim the Solitary, St. Mary the Egyptian, St. Pelagia the Solitary who was saved by St. Bisarioun, St. Jacob the Struggler and St. Augustine.

11. Female Saints:

Reading biographies of female saints, whether martyrs, nuns, servants, or those who deal with spiritual or social activities. Read stories of famous female heroes who are known for their courage and sanctity. These types of stories will change the general idea about women, as some people believe they are just for sexual pleasures and are no good for anything else! Reading these stories might give you an open mind about women because they can do great things in many fields, exactly like men.

12. Practice Humbleness:

Preserve yourself from adulterous fights through practicing humbleness. The divine care abandons us because of pride. However, humility defeats devils. Humble yourself before God, people and yourself. Someone asked St Aghathon about the fight of adultery, so he answered: "Put your weakness before the Lord and you will find rest." St John of the Ladder also says: "If you want to win, don't just fight with your bodily power. Your struggle, vigil and fasting are all in vain if you do not know your weakness and resort to God. It is He who will grant you the grace of chastity."

13. Satisfy Your Love in a Sublime Manner:

Fill your heart with the love it needs. Occupy yourself with social activities, being kind to those who need help, having nice company with faithful friends, live in love with your family members, have mercy on animals or join animal organisations or Ambulance organisations.

14. The Sign of the Cross:

Sign yourself with the Cross frequently. The Cross is the sign of the Lord Jesus Christ, "by whom the world has been crucified to me, and I to the world." (Gal. 6: 14) It is the sign that frightens the devils and make them flee. Sign yourself in true faith, and you will definitely feel the amazing power accompanying the sign of the Cross.

Remedy

We have advised the dear reader to escape and avoid fights of adultery, but what could he do if, out of reluctance or any other reason, he is facing this fight? Here; the cure is divided into various stages according to the level of sin:

1. External Hidden Fights

The heart is the measure of the sexual fights; whether they are at a serious or minor state. Your will is controlling this state. An adulterous thought might come from your senses, your mind or be offered by the devils. If there is no response from the heart, the desire just passes by and disappears. In this stage, a person is still pure and has done no sin, because the thought couldn't stimulate the body, senses or the heart. Although the thought keeps knocking, it is an outside war and is not from within. We can dismiss all these bad thoughts, "Resist the devil and he will flee from you." (James 4: 7)

The adulterous thought wants us to converse with it as this gives it a chance to grow. It is up to your will whether to converse or to shut the door straightaway. Be wise and dismiss the devil because it spoils the heart, mind and body. Don't be deceived by the devil if he tries to convince you to discuss the issue and you don't have to try it if you don't like it. Not everything needs discussion with the devil. If you see a scorpion, you know immediately, what it is, you don't hold it but rather kill it immediately; or at least, run away. But if you carry the scorpion, it will bite you and poison your whole body. It is the same with the thoughts of adultery. St. Ephram the Syrian says, "Rebuke and kick away the devil of adulterous thoughts, exactly as you kick out a dog."

If the thought is direct, you have no excuse for not dismissing it. However, if the thought is veiled and disguised in an innocent form, you need discernment. Remember your previous experiences and fights and learn from your past so as to disclose their reality. An elder once said; "I can't remember the devils deceiving me in the same situation twice."

There may be a certain person about whom you have positive thoughts. Here, the devil starts reminding you of all the good characteristics of the person, then creeps into an unclean relationship. The war of desire then starts. Through previous experience, if you know that thinking deeply about a person's characteristics opens up the gate of desires, you will learn to dismiss these thoughts from the start. Evenmore, you learn to dismiss any thought related to this person totally. We mentioned previously that one's will controls everything, whether it dismisses or accepts the thoughts. However, it depends on the strength of the will.

2. MODERATE INTERNAL FIGHTS

This war starts through two channels: The first channel is when the sexual desire finds acceptance in the heart because of a hidden sexual longing. The second channel is when this thought is rejected by the heart. However, as the thought keeps trying, the will is weakened, and the sexual desire starts finding its way within the person. Both channels, whether because of a hidden desire, or a desire from outside, will lead to one result, which we will discuss. This sinful pleasure is usually very weak at the beginning; With a bit of strong will and a courageous mind, a person can dismiss it and have comfort.

Some Advice:

If this sexual pleasure attacks you because of a certain thought, immediately think of something else, read , pray, sing a hymn or a praise....etc. If you choose to direct your thoughts to a different matter, think about a serious issue which really attracts your concentration. If you think of something trifle, you will go back quickly to your sexual thought. If you choose reading or praying, do it deeply, even if you can't at the beginning. Keep reading or praying until your entire mind is occupied. If you choose to sing a praise or hymn, choose a mournful tune or something that needs accurate muscial note. Choose something you really like and that touches your heart.

• If none of these methods are helping, leave your spot and look at different things. Keep your mind and eyes busy with something else. If still avail, talk to someone and you will definately get rid of the thought because you can't do both at the same time.

• If the thought attacks you while you are listening to someone, talk rather than listen.

• If it attacks while reading, leave the book, even if it is a religious one.

• If the source of this pleasure is a physical one, such as touching, looking or listening, then flee from the whole situation. If you can't, then occupy your mind with something deep. This will disrupt your senses and take their attention off the sexual issue.

• We don't want to recommend a certain way. However, you must choose the strategy that best suits you in escaping the thought and the lust surrounding it.

• Beware of listening to the devil who tries to deceive your mind. When you think of physical pleasure, don't think that you are negotiating with the enemy to overcome him. Even if you win at the end, you have become unclean during the times of negotiations. Although you were trying to dismiss the thought, you were enjoying it. This whole situation contradicts your love to God and contradicts the life of purity. Dismiss the thought quickly without discussion, even if you are trying to negotiate with the enemy to leave you alone. The war is still a light one because the will has authority over the mind. However, time is critical because the will becomes weaker the more you think and negotiate. The angels surrounding you will start abandaning you. The Lord's grace will start to flee. It is all a result of reluctance, in that, you are not dismissing the thought immediately.

This leads to the third stage, which is really dangerous. You are totally condemned before the Lord because you led yourself to this stage, out of your own free will. Here you resemble the children of Israel who disobeyed God by keeping the Canaanites, who later attracted the children of God to the worship of idols. As for you, repeat with the Psalmist, "Early I will destroy all the wicked of the land, that I may cut off all the evildoers from the city of the Lord." (Ps. 101: 8) In this case, the city of the Lord is your heart; the inner Jerusalem.

3. FIERCE INNER FIGHTS

This is the most dangerous stage where the sexual pleasure overcomes the person. He just wants to complete the sinful act as his will can't resist. He is falling between two fierce enemies, one from outside and the other from inside. He knows he is doing something wrong, but can't stop. Many of those who fall into this sin, regret and cry before the Lord because of their weakness.

What can we say, my dear brethren, to those who go through this difficult stage? We are not rebuking you, but we feel sorry you've reached this stage. The Merciful Lord, knows that we are weak human beings, and will have mercy and compassion on you. The most important thing in this stage; don't lose hope. Don't fall into the devil's trap and believe him when he says: "You've already fallen and you have to finish the sin till the end!" Never listen to his gloating. Fight to the best of your will. Flee from the reason of sin and don't try to follow it. Try to mingle with people because in the presence of others, you cannot commit this sin. Try not to sit alone with a person who might be an instrument used by the devil to fight you. In worst cases, it is better to fall alone than to make another sin with you.

DO NOT DESPAIR:

Be sure that even if your whole body is inflamed with sin, you can still gain the crown of struggle from God. He never forgets that you've forbidden your body from a desired pleasure for His sake. In order to win this fierce battle, you need to have a courageous heart. The source of this power is your strong belief that God is with you. He will never deliver you into the hands of your enemy because He cares about your salvation. St Pakhomius, Father of the Community says: "Be of a strong courageous heart from the beginning, so that you might be able to stand before the anger of the dragon. It is very hard if he finds out that you are ready to resist him. He will always try to scare you at the start, so have a strong heart and fight as a mighty warrior against this desire. Put away the weakness of the heart, lest you become lazy and of little faith, giving him the chance to overcome you. Have the heart of a lion".

If you are in your room, have fast access to some verses, saint pictures and holy books so that you are constantly reminded of God.

AFTER THE FALL

There are two kinds of falling; either due to reluctance, or due to weakness. The first kind is a cruel one, because you are willingly depriving yourself of God's grace. As for the second kind, God looks at you kindly and stretches His Hand to uplift you. Usually after the fall, a person feels guilty, regrets his actions and feels disgusted of himself.

Make use of this regret and disgust to start a new clean life. Even if you fall again, do not give up as long as it is out of weakness. There was a monk, living in a monastery, who frequently fell into the sin of adultery. He hated himself yet prayed saying: "My Lord, you can see my sadness and grief, please Lord, whether I like it or dislike it, take me out of this state, because I am like the mud, I love and yearn to sin. You are the Mighty, make me stop this iniquity. It is common that You have mercy on the saints and the righteous because they deserve it, but show the wonder of Your mercies through looking at me. I am the unworthy, yet I have submitted everything between Your Hands." He used to repeat this prayer daily even if he didn't sin. Satan became so furious of his prayers and hope, that he appeared to him face to face and said: "Aren't you ashamed to utter God's holy Name with your defiled mouth?" The monk answered: "You are hitting once and I am hitting once. You are making me fall into sin and I am asking for mercy from God who is Merciful. I will keep fighting you till death and never lose hope in My Lord. I will always be ready for you and at the end, we will see who the winner is; you or God's mercy." Hearing these words, the devil said: "From now on, I will stop fighting you, lest I add to your crowns because of your great hope in your God." The devil departed him since that day, yet the monk kept weeping for his previous sins. If he was tempted with pride, he would remind himself of his many sins. If he was tempted with despair, he would answer, "The mercies of the Lord are so great, He rejoices for the revival of the dead and the return of the prodigal."

Don't yield to the devil if he tries to convince you that the desire is stronger than yourself, and that it is impossible for you to win. It needs time, before you start yielding fruits. Acquiring total chastity and purifying yourself from sin is not an easy matter. It doesn't come suddenly, but rather needs practice and patience. Maintain your hope, increase your prayers, stay away from the causes of sin and you will definitely gain the virtue of chastity. The devil's sole aim of your fall is to make you despair, so that you totally yield to him, believing that your struggle is in vain.

Beware of the devil of shyness that comes straight after the devil of adultery, and forbids you from disclosing the sin to your confession father. This devil is a very tricky one. Just ignore him and confess your sins. We are comforted when we confess certain sins straight after we fall. One of the fathers said that the devil of adultery is defeated immediately after we disclose it. Don't be embarrassed of your confession father; he is also a human being who knows our weaknesses. In addition, he has great experience in this field because of the many confessions of the sort. Be honest in your confession and don't postpone it. You may think it is better for you to calm down first, and then go to confession, but this is a trick from the devil. The situation may worsen or it may happen again and you may get attached to this sin even more.

DREAMS AND WET DREAMS

Wet dreams for males are the release of semen during their sleep. This is accompanied by bad dreams. People should not worry about this because it is not considered a sin; it is just the release of excessive liquid from the body. A defiled dream may precede a wet dream. Although it occurs unwillingly, it is the result of a lustful wish before sleep. The church considers wet dreams as a break from one's fasting and one should not partake of Holy Communion the next morning. According to Leviticus 15, this person is considered defile till evening. He can't enter the altar or touch holy utensils. However, he can participate in the prayers and perform his daily canon. It is preferable to have a shower and change clothes. Wet dreams should be included in confession as well, whether it is frequent or rare. The following are advices concerning this matter:

1. Wet dreams are sometimes the result of stored and oppressed sexual desires. The source might be old memories or news about unclean issues which the mind still remembers. This case needs spiritual remedy such as avoiding the reasons of this sin whenever awake. If a person keeps himself clean and pure while he is awake, it is rare that he will have these unclean dreams, and if he does, he will wake up straight away because he will not be able to stand such a dream.

2. Wet dreams are a result of too much food, especially rich fatty meals. It is also the result of too much sleep or giving the body more rest that what it actually needs. Wet dreams increase if the body relaxes on soft luxurious

beds. However, those who watch during the night and fast properly, rarely have wet dreams.

3. Wet dreams are affected by the position of the body during sleep. They increase if one sleeps on the back, thus warming the spinal cord. They also increase when one sleeps on the abdomen, warming the sexual organs. The best position for sleeping is on the right side.

4. Wet dreams can be reduced by wearing underwear which is a bit loose so as not to press against the sensitive parts of the body.

5. To avoid wet dreams, do not drink too many liquids before sleeping, to avoid filling the bladder.

6. It is better not to go to bed until the body is totally exhausted and needs sleep.

7. Pray a lot before sleeping so that the bed might be holy and the angels surrounding you may preserve your chastity. On the contrary, unclean thoughts which might occupy your mind before sleep, will lead to wet dreams.

8. Do not let the covers rub against your body. Too much coldness will cause the crouching of the body and the pressing of some organs. Too much warmth, leads to wet dreams.

9. Exaggerated fear of wet dreams leads to its occurrence.

10. It could be a result of devilish fights, to agitate you, to prevent you from partaking of Holy Communion, to make you fall in despair, or lead you to adultery. The elderly fathers recommend that you do not remember the

fights you had during your sleep lest they fight you again
while being awake. St John of the Ladder says: "While you
are awake, do not think about the unclean dreams. The
devils' main aim of presenting those dreams is to make you
think about them while you're awake."

IMPORTANT INSTRUCTIONS

1. If the sexual fights are vicious, examine yourself deeply. Discover the reasons behind these fights and remove them. If you can't find a sexual reason, then examine yourself concerning pride and vain glory. Maybe they've crept into your heart, so humble yourself before the Lord that He might take them away. If not, then check if it is from the envy of the devil. The Lord sometimes allows this situation so as to humble you, as said by St. John of the Ladder.

2. A strong courageous heart is one of the basic things which will help you against this sin. High self esteem is very important because a weak heart cannot resist the enemy. Instead, it notices it's weakness, becomes even fiercer and rejoices for its fall.

3. Beware of despair. Fill your heart with hope and dependence on the Lord, believing that His strength helps you defeat this defiled war. Be sure that He will send help even if it is at the fourth part of the night, as He says: "Because he has set his love upon Me, therefore I will deliver him, I will set him on high, because he has known My name. He shall call upon Me, and I will answer him; I will be with him in trouble; I will deliver him and honor him. With long life I will satisfy him, and show him My salvation."(Ps. 91: 14-16) St Ephraim the Syrian says: "Eagles gather around the carcass, and devils gather around a person in despair."

4. Although you are convinced that it is a sin to indulge in and enjoy these sexual thoughts, you may still

be yearning for them. The devil starts working with this initiative to create a situation of despair inside the youth. The devil says, 'If your thoughts are so defiled, what is the use of your struggle?' But even in this case, do not give up. This yearn towards sin is natural as mentioned by St Paul in Romans 7: 23, so "Wait on the Lord, be of good courage, and He shall strengthen your heart. Wait, I say, on the Lord." (Ps. 27: 14) Never doubt that "The Lord is at hand." (Phil 4: 5)

At the start of your spiritual struggle, don't expect yourself to naturally refrain from evil, hate sin and reject desires. These are all high spiritual levels which someone reaches after hard work and forcing oneself in the path of the Spirit. Always put this in your heart: Never despair even in the midst and depth of the worst sin. During this period, cling to the weapons of the Spirit which St. Paul mentions, "Put on the whole armor of God, that you may be able to stand against the wiles of the devil....Stand therefore, having girded your waist with truth, having put on the breastplate of righteousness, and having shod your feet with the preparation of the gospel of peace; above all, taking the shield of faith with which you will be able to quench all the fiery darts of the wicked one. And take the helmet of salvation, and the sword of the Spirit, which is the word of God." (Eph. 6: 10-17)

5. Sometimes the devil uses different tricks to make you fall in sin. He clothes the desire in a garment of virtue so that he might not be exposed immediately, "...and no wonder! For Satan himself transforms himself into an angel of light." (2 Cor. 11: 14) He might clothe sin in the garment of love, mercy or holy zeal for the salvation

of a soul. For example, a youth who volunteers to give a young girl some lessons in a certain subject, or a youth who starts a relationship with a girl who is living in a sinful atmosphere, in an attempt to save her. This situation might start with holy intentions, but the devil might later interfere. We have to do good carefully, lest we lose our spiritual life. Let's flee every evil or semi evil and all the tricks of the evil one.

6. Make sure that you are not alone in the struggle against desires. You have many companions fighting Satan and resisting till bloodshed. Their only motto is, "Yet in all these things we are more than conquerors through Him Who loved us." (Rom.8: 37)

7. Sanctify your thoughts and your body, to be made worthy of wearing holy white clothes. Sing the new song, with the 144,000 celibates, before the Throne of Grace, on top of the Heavenly Zion Mountain. The song about which St John the Theologian says, "and no one could learn that song except the hundred and forty-four thousand who were redeemed from the earth. These are the ones who were not defiled with women, for they are virgins. These are the ones who follow the Lamb wherever He goes." (Rev. 14: 1-4)

PRAYERS

Our Great Holy Lord, Who created man without defilement, on Your likeness and image, to be a holy temple for Yourself, grant me the grace to be pure. Sanctify me so that I become a dwelling place for You. Take off anything which does not please Your Goodness. Purify and cleanse everything in me O my Lord. Extract all the impurity from my heart, purify my senses and preserve my members. Protect me against the desires of the world. You are my Creator Who knows my human weakness. You know all the evil things surrounding me in this world and the stumbles facing me.

Through Your Grace, make me worthy of a pure righteous life. Restrain my desires and give calmness to my body. My Lord God, You ordered the sea and it became silent, now rebuke my desires which hurt my life. I resort to You because I've lost control of my life, amidst the sea of temptations. I come to You, seeking rest under the shadow of Your wings. Shield me within Your protection.

Forgive me for all my sins and iniquities. Do not deal with me according to my sins and ignorance, but forget all about them. Do not deliver me to the hands of my enemies. Watch over my pure life; let it be because of Your grace not because of my power.

Respond to my prayers, O my God, through the prayers of all Your holy saints. Glory be to You forever. Amen.

Prayer

�֍

"Ask, and it will be given to you; seek, and you will find; knock, and it will be opened to you."
(Mt 7:7)

❧ Prayer: Its value and effect

❧ Our need for prayer

❧ Conditions for acceptable prayers

❧ The secret of answered prayers

❧ Encouragements of prayer

❧ Delay in answering prayer

❧ How to pray

❧ Some problems of prayer

❧ Constant prayer

❧ Prayer according to a Discipline

PRAYER: ITS VALUE AND EFFECT

WHAT IS PRAYER?

Do not think my brother that this is an easy question. Do not think that you can answer it easily. The disciples of the Lord needed this knowledge and they asked the Lord one day: "Lord teach us to pray." (Lk 11:1) The saints also defined prayer differently, not as they heard about it or as they read about it, but as they experienced it and tasted it. Descriptions of prayer include: The key to heaven, a cure for the sick, preservation of the healthy, a sharp weapon, a mighty support, a capable intercessor, a trustworthy port, a precious treasure and the work of spiritual people.

St John Chrysostom says, "Prayer is a mighty weapon, a treasure that is always full, a rich man who never falls, a calm marina. It is the source and basis of numerous blessings; It is strong. It is stronger that strength itself."

St Basilius the great defines prayer as "an attachment to God in every instance in life and in all its events. Thus life becomes one prayer that is never interrupted or disturbed."

St Augustine defines it by saying: "It is the key to heaven, as its strength is capable of everything. It protects our souls, and it becomes a source of all virtues, a ladder by which we climb to God, the work of the angels and the basis of faith."

St Isaac the Syrian, who was great in knowledge, defines it according to his experience saying: "Prayer is the constant mentioning of the Lord in the heart of those who fear Him. Our mind is with Him, our conscience is free from all present matters and our heart longs for the expected Hope. Prayer is the pulse of the living will for the Lord. Real prayer is the same as death from the world. Prayer is the mind's cry as it expresses its love for God, it's one heart desire."

Prayer is the tool of a man by which he draws near to God. It is the core of religion, for there is no religion without prayer. It is the oldest and widest spreading ritual; many believe that it is older than sacrifice. From the early eras, people started calling the name of God. Prayer is a natural action and is difficult to describe. It challenges all descriptions for it is deeper than any language. Prayer is the continuous heart beat, the words of our lips, the thoughts of our minds, the actions of our lives. It delivers our souls to the source of grace, to receive the essence of life and peace.

We do not exaggerate the power of prayer as the Lord actually gave it much strength and capability to work, "whatever things you ask in prayer, believing, you will receive." (Mt 21:22) St Paul also directs the believers to its importance and priority by saying: "Therefore I exhort first of all that supplications, prayers, intercessions, and giving of thanks be made for all men, for this is good and acceptable in the sight of God our Saviour." (1 Tim 2:1-3) Also, "Be anxious for nothing, but in everything by prayer and supplication, with thanksgiving, let your requests be made known to God." (Phil 4:6)

Value of Prayer

As we saw earlier, prayer is "very capable," thus it is not strange to realise that the work of prayer is valuable and superior than any other work. Due to its value, the Lord appointed angels to present it to Him, "Then another angel, having a golden censer, came and stood at the altar. He was given much incense, that he should offer it with the prayers of all the saints upon the golden altar which was before the throne. And the smoke of the incense, with the prayers of the saints, ascended before God from the angel's hand." (Rev 8:3,4) St John Chrysostom says, "Prayer is compared to incense because it purifies the spirit from the filth of sin." The angel told Tobia "When you were praying, I presented your prayers before the Lord." (Tobiet 12:12)

St Isaac says, "Individual debate with God is the work of the heavenly hosts. It was revealed to human beings when the Son of God descended to our world and showed us the work of the unseen. Prayer is an elevated work, higher than other virtues, a virtue better than all works." St John Chrysostom says, "When you pray, don't you talk to God? What a privilege is that?!"

Some of the Sayings of the Fathers about the Value of Prayer

St John Chrysostom says, "Contemplate, what a great level of happiness prayer does, what a special honour it has, for you to talk to the Almighty, and converse with Jesus; with it you touch what you desire. There is no tongue that can describe this honour of approaching God and the associated benefits. For if in the world, those who accompany wise men learn from them, and the person who befriends the virtuous people become honourable, then how much more benefits we gain by constant presence before the Lord!! The Psalmist says: Come forward to Him and be enlightened."

He also says, "There is nothing stronger than prayer. Nothing compares to it. A person entering the king's palace and talking privately with him in the presence of all the army officers and others of various positions, will be looked at in a respectable manner; this is like those who pray. Imagine a person entering heaven and courageously moving forward and talking to the King in the presence of the angels, the Seraphim and Cherubim and all the heavenly hosts. What an honour!" He also says, "Prayer is like a water well in the middle of a garden. Without it, everything is dry and unfruitful, and with it, everything is pretty and fruitful."

If prayer has such an honour and ability, then we should thank God for it! If God specified a certain time, once a month to respond to every request, wouldn't we consider this a great blessing?! If an earthly king did that with his people, we would consider this a great present from him? If this is the case, then how about this great blessing from our Lord, that not once a month, but every day and every second He responds to our requests!! David the Prophet said, "Evening and morning and at noon I will pray, and cry aloud, and He shall hear my voice. He has redeemed my soul in peace." (Ps 55:17, 18)

John Cassian says, "Prayer is the support of the three

duties of a Christian person; the first is his relationship with God, the second is his relationship with himself, and the third is his relationship with his relative. We perform our duty towards God in prayer as we call on His name, showing our love, honesty and belief in Him and in acknowledging that He is the source of all blessings. As for our duty towards ourselves, in prayer we search ourselves and evaluate our spiritual person; and towards the relative, we ask and plead for him as for ourselves."

OUR NEED FOR PRAYER

A person is in extreme need to pray for his spiritual and bodily requirements. There is a close relationship between prayer and the life of the spirit. The life of the spirit essentially requires a continuous life of prayer. You can always be under the leadership of the Spirit if you live a continuous life of prayer.

Without prayer, the spiritual life cannot prosper. Through prayer, we receive a cure for all our trespasses; it preserves ourselves in virtue, it is everything in the life of a true believer for it forms an intimate relationship between the Creator and His creation. If we are the branches in the true vine, let us then ensure that we take the necessary food from the original source, otherwise we become dry and fall. This is what we gain in prayer; the blessing of being attached to God. Prayer is a strong rope that links us to God and attracts us to heaven, preventing us from falling and deviating. It takes away all our worries and troubles, and even if we feel lukewarm in prayer, the only cure in again prayer!! Prayer to the spiritual life is like the hand to the body. The hand is a general member of the whole body but it is a tool for itself, serving itself: if the hand is sick, the hand will treat it; if it is dirty, the hand will wash it; and if it is cold, the hand will warm it. Truly, the hand does everything, and so does prayer.

There is a strong similarity between a person breathing and the necessity of prayer for him. Breathing is necessary for the life of the body, just like prayer is necessary for the growth of the spiritual life. If we stop breathing, the result

is the death of the body and if we stop prayer, we face
spiritual death. Breathing is the extension and retraction
of the lungs so that the air enters our bodies; prayer brings
the love of God to enter our spiritual being. However, there
are differences between breathing and prayer. Breathing
is a natural and an automatic operation that requires no
effort; but prayer, needs willpower and effort. It is easier to
breath than not to breath but it is easier not to pray than to
pray. We should learn how to pray, step by step, and force
ourselves to pray.

Just as the wing of a bird tends to fly and the fin of the
fish wants water, the heart of every individual must want
God. A contemporary writer rightfully said: "My heart is
longing for You God, my heart is longing for You! Nothing
in my being longs for You as the longing of my heart.
Other parts of me may be content with your benefits: my
hunger is fulfilled by my daily food, my thirst is satisfied
by the earthly water, my cold is expelled by a heated stove,
my tiredness may be erased by external rest but nothing
external can satisfy my heart." We can notice our need for
prayer by looking into these points:

1. It is the secret for victory:

Without a doubt, prayer is the secret of victory. No one
can dare say that he does not need prayer. If someone says
that, then it means that he does not need God Himself, nor
His care. St John Chrysostom says, "If someone does not
like prayer, know at once that there is nothing good in him
at all. A person who does not pray to God is a dead person
and there is no life in him."

What God intended to give to the souls in His eternal

knowledge, He intended to give through prayer, "Ask and it will be given to you, seek and you will find, knock and it will be opened to you." It is similar to Jacob's ladder that linked earth to heaven, where the angels going up and down represent our requests going up to God and God's blessings coming down to us.

Man is weak and the spiritual enemies are many, so prayer is needed as a defence line!! It is appropriate to repeat the words of Jehoshaphat, king of Judah when the people of Ammon and Moab were against him: "O our God, will You not judge them? For we have no power against this great multitude that is coming against us; nor do we know what to do, but our eyes are upon You." (2 Chr 20:12)

Our Lord Jesus Christ revealed to us the secret of victory on our spiritual enemies when He said "This kind (devil) can come out by nothing but prayer and fasting." (Mk 9:29) The saintly fathers experienced this and say that nothing is more fearful to the devil than seeing someone praying.

It was told about St Tadros the Egyptian that as he was entering his cell, a devil tried to enter but he was tied outside. A second devil came and tried to enter but the saint also tied him outside. A third devil came and saw the other two devils tied and said, "How come you are standing like that outside the cell?" They replied, "There is someone standing inside the cell who is preventing us from entering." This last devil got angry and tried to enter the cell but the saint tied him also by his prayers. The devils were upset from the prayers of the saint and asked him to release them, so the saint said, "Go and be ashamed." They left in great shame.

St Augustine says, "None of those invited can obtain salvation without God's help, and no one deserves this help except through prayer." St John El Daragy, owner of the ladder of virtues, says, "The secret of continuation of grace and virtue, is the continuation of prayer." Whoever leans on the crutch of prayer, will never stumble, for prayer is the support for the one who walks in the righteous path.

A father once said, "Prayer is our means for spiritual development. The Almighty designed the human race and blessed its growth through marriage. The Almighty designed the land to be fertilized and fruitful through farming. Likewise, the Almighty designed our souls to receive numerous blessings through prayer." Thus our Lord Jesus said in the Holy Bible: "Ask and it will be given to you, seek and you will find, knock and it will be opened to you. For everyone who asks receives, and he who seeks finds, and to him who knocks it will be opened."

St Augustine called it 'The key to heaven.' It is true that prayer is a great key that opens all the gates of heaven and all the heavenly treasures. The door of repentance is opened to us by prayer as we receive forgiveness. St Isaac says, "Those who neglect prayer and think that there is another door for repentance, are deceived by the devils." With prayer, the fear of God dwells in our hearts, and the fear of God is the beginning of knowledge. How true is what one of the fathers say: "Whether you are aiming for prayer or for virtue, "Come, you children, listen to me; and I will teach you the fear of the LORD." (Ps 34:11)

Finally, prayer saves us on the great day of judgement.

The Lord Jesus says "But take heed to yourselves, lest your hearts be weighed down with carousing, drunkenness, and cares of this life and that Day come on you unexpectedly. For it will come as a snare on all those who dwell on the face of the whole earth. Watch therefore, and pray always that you may be counted worthy to escape all these things that will come to pass, and to stand before the Son of Man." (Lk 21:34-36)

2. The means to obtain blessings:

Through prayer, we receive blessings of the Holy Spirit. The Lord Jesus says, "If you then, being evil, know how to give good gifts to your children, how much more will your heavenly Father give the Holy Spirit to those who ask Him!" (Lk 11:13) When the Apostles gathered together and prayed, "The place where they were assembled together was shaken; and they were all filled with the Holy Spirit, and they spoke the word of God with boldness." (Acts 4:31)

There is a strong relationship between the Holy Spirit and prayer, for the Holy Spirit is "the spirit of prayer." This is mentioned in Zach 12:10, "And I will pour on the house of David and on the inhabitants of Jerusalem the Spirit of grace and supplication; then they will look on Me." In the Epistles of St Paul, the Holy Spirit was again referred to prayer: "You received the Spirit of adoption by whom we cry out, "Abba, Father" (Rom 8:15); "God has sent forth the Spirit of His Son into your hearts, crying out, "Abba, Father!" (Gal 4:6) The Lord Jesus used the same words "Abba, Father" in his last prayer in Gethsemane. (Mk 14:36)

This is more apparent if we reflect on the words of

St Paul in his Epistle to the Romans "Likewise the Spirit also helps in our weaknesses. For we do not know what we should pray for as we ought, but the Spirit Himself makes intercession for us with groanings which cannot be uttered. Now He who searches the hearts knows what the mind of the Spirit is, because He makes intercession for the saints according to the will of God." (Rom 8: 26, 27) It is clear here that if we were left to ourselves we will not know how to pray but the Spirit of God intervenes and supports us in our weakness. The Spirit "makes intercession for us with groaning which cannot be uttered."

Prayer prepares us for many spiritual blessings. St Isaac the Syrian talks about them:

• Wars mean nothing to the person who prays. Prayer scorns the body, which is the cause of these wars.

• With prayer, the work of repentance is finished, that is self-remorse and sadness. With it, the spirit moves beyond the body and soul. This is what the fathers call spiritual management.

• As one prays continuously, he becomes modest and humble before God. As he yearns to meet God in prayer, pains are afraid to approach him.

• When pure prayer is united with a state of total concentration, then the Word of our Lord is fulfilled when He said: "Whenever two or three are gathered in My Name, I will be in their midst." Meaning the union between soul, body and spirit, or the union between mind, concentration and pure prayer.

• The strength of true prayer burns away one's pains

and evil desires, just like fire.

• Constant dialogue with the Almighty prepares for us a special place with him.

• Through prayer, we attain purity to be able to see God. We cannot receive purity through education or books, but by careful prayer.

• Through prayer, we reach the highest level of virtue and divine love. Without supplication, prayer and many tears, together with vigil and asceticism, divine love cannot be attained.

Thus we see that prayer qualifies us for God's mercy, help and grace. St Paul says, "Let us therefore come boldly to the throne of grace, that we may obtain mercy and find grace to help in time of need." (Heb 4:16) Man is so much in need of God's mercy and grace. All the treasures of mercy and grace are stored for those who ask, "Until now you have asked nothing in My name. Ask, and you will receive, that your joy may be full." (Jn 16:24) Prayer is the way to joy because it makes God a reality. He becomes a strong living truth. There is no greater Joy in heaven or earth other than having an intimate relationship with God. The joy of prayer is mentioned by the Psalmist, "In Your presence is fullness of joy." (Ps 16:11)

We need more time to mention in detail all the blessings of prayer. Truly the Lord specified prayer as the means to win His grace and blessings. St James explains this by saying: "You do not have because you do not ask." (Js 4:2) We need to examine our weaknesses and examine the apathy in our services and ask for God's grace.

3. The Example of the Lord Jesus Christ

The Lord Jesus prayed while He was on earth. The expert Tretliniaws says: "What more should we know about the importance of prayer, Our Lord Himself prayed!!" He did not need prayer for He was given all authority (Mt 28:18), but he left us an example to follow. (1 Pet 2:21)

While He was being baptized, He was praying and the heaven opened up and the Holy Spirit ascended on Him. After healing Simon's mother in law from her fever, He "went out and departed to a solitary place; and there He prayed." (Mk 1:35) Before choosing his twelve disciples "He went out to the mountain to pray, and continued all night in prayer to God." (Lk 6:12) In the transfiguration, "He took Peter, John, and James and went up on the mountain to pray. As He prayed, the appearance of His face was altered, and His robe became white and glistening." (Lk 9:28, 29) Then we read the beautiful prayer of our Lord Jesus in John 17 where He prayed for Himself, His disciples and for all those who will believe in His words.

4. The Example of the Apostles themselves:

The apostles, the disciples of the Lord, the leaders of the first church, had prayer as their priority. When they wanted to choose another disciple instead of Judas the betrayer, they prayed and the lot fell on Matthias. (Acts 1:24-26) After the coming of the Holy Spirit in the Pentecost, they were steadfast in their prayers. (Acts 2:42) After healing the lame man and the threats of the chief priests, "They raised their voice to God with one accord... And when they had prayed, the place where they were assembled together was shaken; and they were all filled with the Holy Spirit, and they spoke the word of God with boldness." (Acts 4:24-30) When their duties increased, they thought to appoint seven deacons, "It is not desirable that we should leave the word of God and serve tables. Therefore, brethren, seek out from among you seven men...whom we may appoint over this business; but we will give ourselves continually to prayer and to the ministry of the word." (Acts 6:2-4) When Herod arrested St Paul and put him in jail and was about to kill him, it is written in Acts, "Peter was therefore kept in prison, but constant prayer was offered to God for him by the church." (Acts 12:5) When Peter was rescued by an angel and went to the house of Mary, the mother of St Mark, "many were gathered together praying." (Acts 12:12) We can now understand that the strength of the early church came from strong prayer.

St Paul's Epistles are full of worship, supplication and thanksgiving. These Epistles reflect how his prayers lifted him up to the presence of God, even during the toughest times of his life. St Paul reached a high level in prayer, for God sent him many revelations and answered many of his prayers, "For there stood by me this night an angel of God to whom I belong and whom I serve, saying, 'Do not be afraid, Paul; you must be brought before Caesar; and indeed God has granted you and all those who sail with you." (Acts 27:23,24)

When we look at the life of this apostle, we find that he was in a constant relationship with God, feeling His presence all the time. St Paul was talking out of his own experience when he recommended the faithful Thessalonians to "pray without ceasing and in everything to give thanks." (1 Thes

5:17) When St Paul was imprisoned in Philippe, he stayed up the whole night in prayer and praise. Then there was a great earthquake and the foundations of the prison were shaken. Immediately the prison doors were opened and everyone's chains were loosed!!

Paul prayed for himself, for others, for the churches he established, for all the tribes of Israel and for all human beings. "For God is my witness, whom I serve with my spirit in the gospel of His Son, that without ceasing I make mention of you always in my prayers." (Rom 1:9,10) "Therefore I also, after I heard of your faith in the Lord Jesus and your love for all the saints, do not cease to give thanks for you, making mention of you in my prayers." (Eph 1:15,16) "For this reason we also, since the day we heard it, do not cease to pray for you." (Col 1:9) "Night and day praying exceedingly that we may see your face and perfect what is lacking in your faith." (1 Thes 3:10) "I thank God, whom I serve with a pure conscience, as my forefathers did, as without ceasing I remember you in my prayers night and day." (2 Tim 1:3)

THE POWER OF PRAYER

Without a doubt, prayer is very powerful as the forefathers, prophets and Apostles all experienced it. Connecting to God and the unseen world is not only a realistic event for those who pray but it is also accompanied with strength "But those who wait on the LORD shall renew their strength; they shall mount up with wings like eagles, they shall run and not be weary, they shall walk and not faint." (Is 40:31)

When a person is connected to God through true prayer, he is enlightened and receives strength to do anything, works that Jesus did and greater. (John 14:12) When a person holds on to God in prayer, God holds on to him, "Deep calls unto deep at the noise of Your waterfalls; all Your waves and billows have gone over me." (Psalm 42:7) Our misery calls on the mercies of God. We understand the strength of prayer from its nature, our experience and from the testimony of the Word of God.

In the Old Testament, God spoke to Moses the prophet regarding the poor, "And it will be that when he cries to Me, I will hear, for I am gracious." (Ex 22:27) He gave Solomon this great promise after he built the temple, "I have heard your prayer, and have chosen this place for Myself as a house of sacrifice...if My people who are called by My name will humble themselves, and pray and seek My face, and turn from their wicked ways, then I will hear from heaven, and will forgive their sin and heal their land. Now My eyes will be open and My ears attentive to prayer made in this place." (2 Chron 7:12-15)

The Psalms are full of Divine promises emphasizing the strength of prayer:

(Psalm 9:12, 10:7, 34:15, 37:4, 56:9, 62:2-5, 69:33, 81:1, 86:5, 91:15, 102:17, 145:18)

"He shall regard the prayer of the destitute, and shall not despise their prayer...For He looked down from the height of His sanctuary; from heaven the LORD viewed the earth, to hear the groaning of the prisoner." (Psalm 102:17-20) Whoever looks into the writings of Isaiah, Jeremiah, Ezekiel, Joel, Amos, Zephaniah and Zachariah will find it full of great and precious promises for those who pray.

The New Testament also emphasises the power of prayer and the promises available for those who pray:

• "Ask, and it will be given to you; seek, and you will find; knock, and it will be opened to you. For everyone who asks receives, and he who seeks finds, and to him who knocks it will be opened." (Matt 7:7,8)

• "Or what man is there among you who, if his son asks for bread, will give him a stone? Or if he asks for a fish, will he give him a serpent? If you then, being evil, know how to give good gifts to your children, how much more will your Father who is in heaven give good things to those who ask Him!" (Matt 7:9-11)

• "If two of you agree on earth concerning anything that they ask, it will be done for them by My Father in heaven." (Matt 18:19)

• "Whatever things you ask in prayer, believing, you will receive." (Matt 18:19)

• "Whatever you ask the Father in My name He will give you." (John 16:23)

Believers across the ages found grace helping in time of need. (Heb 4:16) They prayed for themselves, for others and for the church, for they knew that "The effective, fervent prayer of a righteous man avails much." (James 5:16) How many miracles happened and are still happening through prayer? There are more answered prayers written in the Holy Bible than promises made. Abraham, Jacob, Moses, Gideon, David, Isaiah, Elisha, Ezekiel, Daniel, Jeremiah and several others, can witness to the power of prayer in their lives.

CONDITIONS OF ACCEPTED PRAYERS

In order for a prayer to be accepted, there are a few points to consider:

1. From a pure heart:

A pure heart is the temple of God and the dwelling of the Father, the Son, and the Holy Spirit. There are obstacles for prayer, as mentioned by St Peter who says, "That your prayers may not be hindered." (1 Peter 3:7) Probably the hidden lusts in the heart are one of the most important factors that hinders prayer. St Neels El Sinaiy says, "A chained man cannot run, and a mind that is associated with desires cannot see spiritual prayer for it will always be attracted and distracted by sensual ideas." Whenever we have lusts in our heart, we start worshipping these idols, instead of worshipping God in true prayer. Isaiah the prophet expressed this: "Behold, the LORD's hand is not shortened, that it cannot save; nor His ear heavy, that it cannot hear. But your iniquities have separated you from your God; and your sins have hidden His face from you, so that He will not hear." (Is 59:1,2) Ezekiel also expressed this by saying, "Son of man, these men have set up their idols in their hearts...Should I let Myself be inquired of at all by them?" (Ez 14:3)

A pure heart is not only pure from sin, but it is the heart that is not divided. This means that the love of the world does not divide or separate it from the love of God. This is what the Lord meant when He said: "And you will seek Me

and find Me, when you search for Me with all your heart."
(Jer 29:13) David the prophet says: "With my whole heart
I have sought You." (Psalm 119:10) Many blessings are
received if our prayer comes from a pure heart. St Isaac
says, "If an altar is not consecrated, the bread on it will
be mere bread and not the living sacrifice of the Body and
Blood of Christ. Likewise, the inner altar of our heart needs
to be pure so as to welcome the presence of the Holy Spirit
within us."

2. According to the will of God:

John the Beloved says: "If we ask anything according
to His will, He hears us." (1 John 5:14) This means that
anything we ask should be in accordance with His love and
wisdom. The Lord who ordered us to ask, and promised to
respond, will not abandon His wisdom for our ignorance
when we ask for something that is not good for us!! For
"we do not know what we should pray for as we ought."
(Rom 8:26) Sometimes we pray for something that appears
right in our own eyes, but the Lord does not respond. Later,
we realize that it was better that the Lord did not give us
what we asked for.

This is similar to a child who cries for a dangerous and
sharp tool but the father, out of his love, will not give it to
him. St John Chrysostom says, "God knows the exact hour
when He gives us what is useful for us. A child shouts,
objects and is upset wanting to hold a knife, but due to
the love of his parents, they refuse to give it to him. This
is exactly how God treats us. He then gives us better than
what we ask for."

There is another point that St Paul draws our attention to. In our weakness and blindness, we find the support of the Holy Spirit who "makes intercession for the saints." The Holy Spirit, who is God, intercedes for us, according to the will of God. "Now He who searches the hearts knows what the mind of the Spirit is, because He makes intercession for the saints according to the will of God." (Rom 8:27)

Some people wonder why they should pray if God already knows what they need and has already organised everything according to his will. But the Lord Jesus taught us to persist in prayer all the time, as seen when he was talking about the widow and the unjust judge. The Lord Jesus also prayed in the garden of Gethsemane, just before His suffering. He asked His Father three times to "take this cup away from Me; nevertheless not My will, but Yours, be done." (Luke 22:42) Let us present our requests to God and say "not my will but Yours be done." We should say it with a heart full of submission. The Lord also taught us this in the Father's prayer, "Your will be done on earth as it is in heaven."

3. In the name of our Lord Jesus:

The Lord Jesus commanded the disciples to ask things "in His Name." Consequently, their prayers were answered. "Whatever you ask in My name, that I will do." (John 14:13,14) "Whatever you ask the Father in My name, He may give you." (John 15:16) "Until now you have asked nothing in My name. Ask, and you will receive, that your joy may be full." (John 16:24) "In that day you will ask in My name." (John 16:26)

Not only is the request presented in His Blessed Name,

but also the response is given by the strength of His Holy Name. In John 16:26, the Lord says "In that day you will ask in My name." This expression refers to the day of descent of the Holy Spirit. For without the Spirit of God, we cannot do anything. In the beginning, everybody waited for the Pentecost and now everybody depends on the work of the Spirit inside man. Everything depends on the Holy Spirit and without the Holy Spirit we cannot even confess that Jesus is our Lord for "no one can say that Jesus is Lord except by the Holy Spirit." (1 Cor 12:3)

What does it mean praying in the name of Jesus and why should I pray in His name? Before salvation and reconciliation, man was in a state of animosity with God but through the death of His Son, we were made worthy to inherit eternal life. Every time we sin, we break this reconciliation with Christ for "the wages of sin is death." (Rom 6:23) So although we do not deserve salvation, the Lord gives it to us through the power of His death and His Holy name. Consequently, he gives us the power to ask and receive anything through His name and we should not lose this opportunity. It is similar to a man who goes to a bank without a cheque. The banker will never give this customer money. However, with a cheque, the customer is able to receive money. We do not deserve anything from our Heavenly Father, but He has paid a cheque through His blood, allowing us all to receive eternal life and ask anything in His name.

Thus the church presents all its requests this way: "in Jesus Christ Our Lord" and "through the grace, loving kindness of your only Begotten Son, Our Lord and Saviour Jesus Christ..." Our Lord Jesus gave us the gift of using

His Name when we present our requests to the Heavenly Father so that we may receive all our needs.

4. In total obedience:

The Lord says "And whatever we ask we receive from Him, because we keep His commandments and do those things that are pleasing in His sight." (1 John 3:22) Therefore, the secret to answered prayer is a life of obedience and submission to the Lord's commandments.

We often question the power of prayer because we do not always receive what we ask for. The reason is that we do not keep His commandments and do those things that are pleasing in His sight. Jesus says: "My food is to do the will of Him who sent Me, and to finish His work." (John 4:34) Very nice words were uttered by St Paul about the Lord Jesus, "Then I said, 'Behold, I have come— in the volume of the book it is written of Me, to do Your will, O God." (Heb 10:7)

5. By complete faith:

St James says: "If any of you lacks wisdom, let him ask of God, who gives to all liberally and without reproach, and it will be given to him. But let him ask in faith, with no doubting, for he who doubts is like a wave of the sea driven and tossed by the wind. For let not that man suppose that he will receive anything from the Lord." (James 1:5-7) These words are a practical explanation for the words of the Lord "For assuredly, I say to you, whoever says to this mountain, 'Be removed and be cast into the sea,' and does not doubt in his heart, but believes that those things he says will be done, he will have whatever he says. Therefore I say to you, whatever things you ask when you pray, believe that you receive them, and you will have them." (Mark 11:23, 24) This is what St Paul meant in his epistle to the Hebrews "Let us therefore come boldly to the throne of grace, that we may obtain mercy and find grace to help in time of need." (Heb 4:17) This trust in God is a form of faith. (Heb 11:1)

Prayer without faith is obsolete. Faith is not the greatest virtue for it was said: "though I have all faith, so that I could remove mountains, but have not love, I am nothing." (1 Cor 13:2) However, faith is the first virtue. Faith without love is nothing; but love without faith is impossible for I cannot love someone if I do not trust him. When we do not get what we ask for, we should wait until God's purpose is revealed. For "It is not for you to know times or seasons which the Father has put in His own authority." (Acts 1:7) If our faith is true, it will bring with it patience.

There is a lot written on faith, "for whatever is not from faith is sin" (Rom 14:23); "But without faith it is impossible to please Him." (Heb 11:6) Faith is powerful and prayer without faith has no strength. If you sought help from a powerful man, but inwardly, you doubted that he could help, this would be an insult to the powerful man. Similarly, when you go to God in prayer, trust that He is a powerful God who is capable of performing all things. Remind yourself, "May He grant you according to your heart's desire." (Psalm 20:4)

St John El Dargy says, "Faith is the wing of prayer and without it, the prayer will return to the person again." John Cassaian says, "Wretched is the person who prays without believing." St Augustine says, "If faith is absent, there will be no effective prayer because you will never call on someone if you do not believe in them." Similarly, the apostle says "whoever calls on the name of the LORD shall be saved." (Rom 10:13) He also says: "How then shall they call on Him in whom they have not believed?" (Rom 10:14) Thus we should believe in prayer and have faith in its power. Faith derives prayer, and the spring of prayer gives strength. The Lord Jesus says, "Rise and pray, lest you enter into temptation," (Luke 22:46) for any temptation is the outcome of being far from faith!! Thus says the Lord "Simon, Simon! Indeed, Satan has asked for you, that he may sift you as wheat. But I have prayed for you, that your faith should not fail." (Luke 22:31,32)

6. With thanksgiving:

Thanksgiving to the Lord was ordered many times in the Holy Bible. It occurred numerous times in the Old Testament and the Jews were required to present a sacrifice of thanksgiving among their offerings presented in the temple. This was also repeated in the New Testament.

God grieves when He does not receive thanksgiving. An unthankful heart is a sin of many. When the Lord Jesus healed the ten lepers and only one came back to thank Him, He said in pain, "Were there not ten cleansed? But where are the nine?" (Luke 17:17) How many times does the Lord look at us sadly because we forget to thank Him for His many blessings. St Paul always taught his believers the importance of thanksgiving as he mentioned it alot in his writings. He urged the believers in Ephesus to "give thanks always for all things." (Eph 5:20) Later he mentioned, "in everything give thanks; for this is the will of God in Christ Jesus for you." (1 Thess 5:18) He told the Colossians to be "rooted and built up in Him and established in the faith, as you have been taught, abounding in it with thanksgiving." (Col 2:7) Thanksgiving is part of prayer; "Continue earnestly in prayer, being vigilant in it with thanksgiving." (Col 4:2) St Paul wrote to the Philippians, "Be anxious for nothing, but in everything by prayer and supplication, with thanksgiving, let your requests be made known to God." (Phil 4:6) On this depends a precious promise "and the peace of God, which surpasses all understanding, will guard your hearts and minds through Christ Jesus." (Phil 4:7)

We never thank God for His numerous blessings yet we remember to thank others for their deeds of kindness. We express our gratitude to people in many ways, which is good, but we should first give thanks to the One who gives us abundantly. Our church teaches us the importance of thanksgiving by praying the thanksgiving prayer at the beginning of all its worships and prayers. We start with the Thanksgiving prayer in the holy liturgy, in marriages, funerals, baptisms and the raising of incense, "Let us give thanks to the beneficent and merciful God...for He has protected, assisted, preserved, accepted us, had compassion upon us, supported us and brought us to this hour...we thank You on every occasion, in every condition and for all things."

Thanking God involves acknowledging His love, care, mercy, and wisdom. It is an announcement of submitting life to Him. St Neels el Siani says, "Prayer is the expression of joy and thanksgiving." We should always have a spirit of thanksgiving. St Paul commands his disciple Timothy to "Exhort first of all that supplications, prayers, intercessions, and giving of thanks be made for all men...For this is good and acceptable in the sight of God our Savior." (1 Tim 2:1-3) We should not forget to thank God for every gift, but rather, give thanks to God in every prayer you say. Our continual thanksgiving will encourage God to give us more. St Isaac says, "A gift that is not increased is that which lacks thanksgiving."

Let us not only thank God for the things we asked for and received, but also for the things we asked for and did not receive. In this case, we thank God for His wisdom. St John Chrysostom says, "If we receive what we asked for or if we did not receive what we asked for, we should still keep praying, for we do not know what is good for us, but God alone knows. We should consider receiving or not receiving as the equivalent blessing and thank God for this."

All the men of prayer, whether in the Holy Bible or in the history of the church, were men who always gave thanks to God. For example, David the prophet showed the spirit of thanksgiving in many of his psalms. "Bless the LORD, O my soul; and all that is within me, bless His holy name!" (Psalm 103:1); "I will sing of the mercies of the LORD forever; with my mouth will I make known Your faithfulness to all generations." (Psalm 89:1); "I will extol You, my God, O King; and I will bless Your name forever and ever. Every day I will bless You, and I will praise Your name forever and ever." (Psalm 145:1,2)

7. With forgiveness:

In the ideal prayer that the Lord gave to His disciples, He explained that we cannot ask God for forgiveness of our sins without having forgiven those who sinned against us.

In the sermon on the mount, the Lord taught us to pray: "And forgive us our debts, as we forgive our debtors." (Matt 6:12) After this ideal prayer, the Lord continued: "For if you forgive men their trespasses, your heavenly Father will also forgive you. But if you do not forgive men their trespasses, neither will your Father forgive your trespasses." (Matt 6:14,15) The Lord Jesus repeated this another time, when He said: "And whenever you stand praying, if you have anything against anyone, forgive him, that your Father in heaven may also forgive you your trespasses. But if you do not forgive, neither will your Father in heaven forgive your trespasses." (Mark 11:25,26). St Neels El Siniai says, "Those who pray while they have hatred and sadness inside them, are like those who are pouring water in a bucket with holes."

THE SECRET OF ANSWERED PRAYERS

We previously talked about the conditions for acceptable prayers and we mentioned some of the essential points for acceptable prayers. Here we want to add a few more points that strengthen prayer and its speedy answer.

FIRST: HUMILITY

One of the things that strengthen prayer and its effect on God is the humility of a person before God. Humility can come in many forms, like humiliating the heart and mind, fasting, bowing (metania) or shedding tears. Joel the prophet says: "Now, therefore," says the LORD, "Turn to Me with all your heart, with fasting, with weeping, and with mourning." So rend your heart, and not your garments; return to the LORD your God, for He is gracious and merciful, slow to anger, and of great kindness; and He relents from doing harm." (Joel 2:12,13)

1. Humility:

The Lord answered the requests of Daniel because of his humility. Daniel prayed for Jerusalem and for all the people who were in bondage; "Then I set my face toward the Lord God to make request by prayer and supplications, with fasting, sackcloth, and ashes. And I prayed to the LORD my God, and made confession, and said, "O Lord, great and awesome God we have sinned and committed iniquity, we have done wickedly and rebelled, even by departing from Your precepts and Your judgments...O Lord, righteousness belongs to You, but to us shame of face...O Lord, to us belongs shame of face, to our kings, our princes, and our fathers, because we have sinned against You..."O Lord, according to all Your righteousness, I pray, let Your anger and Your fury be turned away from Your city Jerusalem, Your holy mountain; because for our sins, and for the iniquities of our fathers, Jerusalem and Your people are a reproach to all those around us. Now therefore, our God, hear the prayer of Your servant, and his supplications...for we do not present our supplications before You because of our righteous deeds, but because of Your great mercies. O Lord, hear! O Lord, forgive! O Lord, listen and act..." (Dan 9:3-19)

Daniel continued in this humility for three weeks; he did not eat delicious food, or eat meat or drink wine or anoint himself until the angel Gabriel appeared to him and said: "Do not fear, Daniel, for from the first day that you set your heart to understand, and to humble yourself before your God, your words were heard; and I have come because of your words." (Dan 10:12)

Ahab, the evil king whom the bible said about him: "But there was no one like Ahab...So it was when Ahab heard those words that Elijah the prophet spoke about what would happen to him and his house that "he tore his clothes and put sackcloth on his body, and fasted and lay in sackcloth, and went about mourning. And the word of the LORD came to Elijah the Tishbite, saying, "See how Ahab has humbled himself before Me? Because he has humbled himself before Me, I will not bring the calamity in his days. In the days of his son I will bring the calamity on his house." (1 Kings 21:27-29)

Thus we can see the effect of humility in prayer:

St John Chrysostom says, "The tax collector cried with a humble heart: God, be merciful to me a sinner... (Luke 18:13), so he was justified rather than the Pharisee. Here the humble prayer is better than a righteous deed done without humility! The Pharisee showed off his righteousness by his fasting and giving regular tithes, while the tax collector presented a broken heart without deeds. The Lord does not listen to words but listens to the feelings of the heart."

St Isaac says, "The Grace of God always stands afar, watching man during his prayer. If it notices a humble thought, it will immediately come with all the support. Thus, the devil tries to attack to prevent humble thoughts during prayer."

Isaiah the prophet says, "But on this one will I look: On him who is poor and of a contrite spirit, and who trembles at My word." (Is 66:2)

Humility before God does not mean repeating the usual expressions: we are sinners and unworthy. Humility is to truly feel this in our hearts, to feel all our sins, insults and shortcomings towards our Almighty Lord, and to attribute whatever is good in us to the Lord for every good gift, and every perfect talent is from above. When we approach God in prayer, we should fill our hearts and minds with these feelings. St Isaac says, "If you stand praying before God, become like an ant in your mind, like a fly, like a child before the Lord, to be prepared for the parental care provided for children by their fathers."

2. Fasting:

We dedicated part of this book to fasting and talked about the relationship between fasting and prayer. We read many parts in the Holy Bible where it links prayer with fasting. It is enough what the Lord Almighty says, "This kind (the devil) can come out by nothing but prayer and fasting." (Mark 9:29) Without a doubt, fasting is an important tool and when prayer is added, it is stronger. St Isaac says, "If the body is weakened by fasting and humbleness, the soul is encouraged by the prayer of the spirit."

3. Prostrations (metanias):

Prostrations (metanias) is the strongest means to show our humility before God. The word 'metania' originally means repentance in Greek. Prostration is a true expression of submission and humility where the body and the spirit share in worshipping God. The Lord Jesus says, "for the Father is seeking such to worship Him." (John 4:23) Also St Paul says, "that at the name of Jesus every knee should bow, of those in heaven, and of those on earth, and of those under the earth." (Phil 2:10) This was expressed by St Cyril in his Liturgy, "O Prince of Life and King of Ages, God unto whom every knee bows, of those in heaven, of those on earth, and of those under the earth; to whom everything is subject and in the bond of servitude, bowing their heads to the sceptre of Thy kingdom."

Prostraions should be accompanied by short prayers. For example if a young man is defeated by his body, he may say, "My Lord Jesus Christ have mercy upon me, help me, and give calmness to my body," or "My Lord Jesus Christ, end the restlessness of my body," or "My Lord Jesus Christ, purify my heart, thought, body, and secure my organs," or "I have sinned against You My Lord Jesus Christ, have mercy upon me and break away the strength of the devil."

St Isaac says, "There is nothing more loved by God, honoured by angels, feared by demons, that defeats sin, attracts mercy, brings humbleness, governs the heart, brings consolation, and renews the mind, than finding the believer who is always bowing to the ground in prayer." John Saba the spiritual elder says, "Force yourself to bow before God as this is the motive for prayer. Do not think that bowing before God is an easy matter. If thoughts interrupt us during prayer and we feel bored, let us bow to the ground with the prayer book in our hands and supplicate to God to give us energy to continue our prayer."

While describing the monks of Egypt, John Cassian says: "After finishing a psalm, they would bow to the ground humbly, while saying a short prayer. They would stand up again in great piety and devoutness, while all their thoughts are still held in prayer."

St Basilius the Great says, "Whenever we bow to the ground, we refer to how sins lowered us to the ground; and when we stand upright, we confess the Lord's grace and mercy that raised us up from the ground to have a place in heaven."

We should note here that the praying person should not practice bowing as he wishes. This spiritual exercise should be done under the guidance of the spiritual father.

4. Tears:

Finally we reach the mighty undefeated weapon of "tears." God the Almighty is conquered by tears. The bridegroom told the bride in the Song of Songs "Turn your eyes away from me, for they have overcome me." (Song of Songs 6:5) The eyes that look towards God can never be disappointed. David was a man of prayer and experienced tears and knew its strength. He often tells us about tears in his Psalms... "I am weary with my groaning; All night I make my bed swim; I drench my couch with my tears;" (Psalm 6:6) "The LORD has heard the voice of my weeping;" (Psalm 6) "Hear my prayer, O LORD, and give ear to my cry; do not be silent at my tears;" (Psalm 39:12) "Because zeal for Your house has eaten me up, and the reproaches of those who reproach You have fallen on me. When I wept and chastened my soul with fasting... I also made sackcloth my garment;" (Psalm 69:9-11) "Put my tears into Your bottle; are they not in Your book?" (Psalm 56:8)

Throughout all ages, the men of God used tears in humiliation to obtain their requests from God. Job used the weapon of tears, "I have sewn sackcloth over my skin, and laid my head in the dust. My face is flushed from weeping." (Job 16: 15-16) Ezra also prayed while weeping and bowing in front of the house of God. The people also wept bitterly with him. (Ezra 10:1) Jeremiah, the weeping prophet, wrote the book of Lamentations and he wished for tears "Oh, that my head were waters, and my eyes a fountain of tears, that I might weep day and night." (Jer 9:1) Hezekiah the king of Judea wept bitterly when he was sick and the answer of the Lord came through Isaiah the prophet, "I have heard your prayer, I have seen your tears;

surely I will heal you." (2 Kings 20:1-5) The Psalmist made it a general rule for joy and happiness, "Those who sow in tears shall reap in joy." (Psalm 126:5) The Lord Himself invited us through Joel the prophet saying: "Turn to Me with all your heart, with fasting, with weeping, and with mourning." (Joel 2:12)

The Lord blessed the weeping eyes, "Blessed are you who weep now." (Luke 6:21) He had compassion on the widow of Nain who lost her only son and He told her "Do not weep." (Luke 7:13) The sinner woman who bowed, crying at Jesus' feet, deserved the forgiveness of her sins. (Luke 7:27) Also the disciple Peter, who denied his Master, was forgiven after crying bitterly.

As for the relationship between tears and prayer, John El Daragy says, "Tears is the mother and daughter of prayer!! For tears lead us to the chamber of prayer and it is also a gift of humble prayer. But let us beware of pride in this case." St Ouggreec says, "If you have tears in your prayers, do not be of proud heart as if you are better than all others. For tears were given to you by the Lord to assist you in confessing your sins. Do not exchange this support by pains that may offend Your Giver." There is much that the saints have said about tears.

St Ephraim the Syrian says, "Pour tears before God so that your prayers become like incense. Running water is for fire and running tears is for the time of temptation. Water will put off the fire and tears will stop the evil lust." John El Daragy says, "A weeping eye is a constant tub for the baptism of repentance and renewal." St Isaac says, "Blessed are those who weep for righteousness for they will always see the Face of God." St Oughreec also says,

"Use tears when you are asking for something you desire, for the Lord is very happy with the prayers that are full of tears and is glad and quick to accept it."

Tears do a lot; it prevents the wrath of God, it saves one from troubles, it rescues one from death and attracts the souls that are far. A good example is St Monica who cried for the salvation of her son, Augustine. St Ambrosius, Bishop of Milan, told her, "Woman, trust that the son of these tears can never perish!!" Thus the church asks its children to call for tears from God. This is expressed in the second service of midnight prayer where the praying person says, "Give me, Lord, fountains of many tears as You did in the past to the sinful woman. Make me worthy to shed my tears on Your feet which took me to the right path..."

SECOND: PERSEVERANCE AND PERSISTENCE

God promised to answer our requests if we present them faithfully, but sometimes we feel He is slow in responding. This is because God wants us to persevere in our requests so as to attain many virtues and become men of prayer. Perseverance and persistence are expressions of faith and nothing gladdens God's Heart more than faith. The woman from Canaan persevered before the Lord for the sake of her sick daughter. As a result of her perseverance, Jesus did not disappoint her; on the contrary He praised her behaviour by saying: "O woman, great is your faith! Let it be to you as you desire." (Matt 15:28)

Our Lord Jesus teaches us perseverance in two parables. The first parable is that of the midnight friend.

(Luke 11:5-8)

"Which of you shall have a friend, and go to him at midnight and say to him, 'Friend, lend me three loaves; for a friend of mine has come to me on his journey, and I have nothing to set before him'; and he will answer from within and say, 'Do not trouble me; the door is now shut, and my children are with me in bed; I cannot rise and give to you?' I say to you, though he will not rise and give to him because he is his friend, yet because of his persistence he will rise and give him as many as he needs." The Lord concluded this parable with clear words: "So I say to you, ask, and it will be given to you; seek, and you will find; knock, and it will be opened to you." (Lk 11: 5-9)

The second parable is the parable of the widow and the unjust judge. It talks about how persistence weakens the devil. St Luke introduced it by saying: "Then He spoke a parable to them, that men always ought to pray and not lose heart, saying: "There was in a certain city a judge who did not fear God nor regard man. Now there was a widow in that city; and she came to him, saying, 'Get justice for me from my adversary.' And he would not for a while; but afterward he said within himself, 'Though I do not fear God nor regard man, yet because this widow troubles me I will avenge her, lest by her continual coming she weary me." Then the Lord said, "Hear what the unjust judge said. And shall God not avenge His own elect who cry out day and night to Him, though He bears long with them? I tell you that He will avenge them speedily." (Luke 18:1-8)

There are so many blessings that the Lord clarified in this parable. The Lord is comparing Himself with the unjust judge who avenged the widow because of her persistence.

He shows that He will certainly respond to those who persist in their requests. If the unjust judge responded, will the Lord not respond?! Jesus answered this question saying: "He will avenge them speedily."

St Augustine comments on the parable of the unjust judge saying: "Our Lord Jesus who is with us will not encourage us in such a way unless He is ready to give. He is ready to give more than we are ready to receive. If the Lord is not ready to give, He would not have given us this parable about persistence. If the unjust judge helped the widow, how much more will the Lord, who is full of love, mercy and compassion, give to us."

Persistence is a necessary virtue and without it we cannot obtain other virtues like patience. (James 1:4) St Basilius the great says, "If your request is according to the will of God, then do not stop asking until you receive it. Our Lord Himself mentioned that in the parable of the man who persistently asked his friend for bread in the middle of the night; we must not be bored from our prayers even if it lasts for years and even if our requests seem impossible, for nothing is impossible with God." He also says, "God knows what we need and He gives us our bodily needs without us asking, for he makes the sun shine on the righteous and the wicked. As for faith, righteousness, virtue, or the heavenly kingdom, He slows in answering so that man does not obtain it except by asking and pleading with effort and patience. This is because the Lord wants us to love goodness and seek it. When we obtain it, He wants us to hold onto it."

St Isaac says, "If you are void of the virtue of perseverance, do not expect to receive real comfort in your prayers, for perseverance means work. Without perseverance, you will not bear the fruits of prayer or fasting or vigil. The possibility of falling must always be in front of our eyes and that is why God encouraged us to pray continuously and persist on asking and requesting." St Isaac also says, "Sometimes we ask from God and do not receive, and this is just, for we do not ask continuously and patiently with trust. God does not respond quickly to our requests so that we may knock again on His door and persist on our request."

ENCOURAGEMENTS OF PRAYER

SILENCE

The first element that encourages prayer is inward and outward silence. A person who lives in continuous noise does not know how to pray properly. A person whose heart is full of thoughts and various lusts, cannot pray as he should. Thus, silence, solitude and calmness are essential.

Outward silence is important as the Lord Jesus Himself often went alone to a secluded area to pray, "And when He had sent the multitudes away, He went up on the mountain by Himself to pray." (Matt 14:23) St John Chrysostom says: "Why did he go up on the mountain? To teach us that solitude is essential when we pray to God. We always see Him leaving to the wilderness, and spending the night praying, teaching us to search for quietness in our prayers, for the wilderness is the mother of solitude (calmness). It is the quiet port that saves us from our troubles."

There is a great story in the Paradise of the Desert Fathers about a novice who went to his teacher complaining of lack of concentration and comfort in his prayers. The experienced elder brought a pot and poured water into it and then dropped a small stone which made some waves in the water. He then ordered his disciple to look into the water and asked him what he saw. The disciple answered that he saw shades. The teacher waited until the water became calm and asked his disciple to look again and to tell him what he saw. He answered that he saw his face as if in a mirror. Then the teacher told the novice: "Go my son, be calm with yourself and you will be comforted in prayer."

That is why the saints loved silence and enjoyed living in quietness. The Lord Jesus says: "Whenever you pray, go to your room and close your door." St Augustine comments on this verse by saying: "Our rooms are our hearts, as mentioned in the Psalms. "Meditate within your heart on your bed and be still." (Psalm 4:4) It is easy to go into our actual room but what is meant here is our inner rooms."

John Cassian says, "What is the meaning of the closed door in prayer? Isn't it the calmness and total silence of the soul and the humble lips before the Observer of hearts?! If prayer is mixed with silence, it will have many spiritual fruits."

St Isaac says, "Through silence, one obtains humbleness, patience, inner illumination, salvation from temptation, spiritual gifts, thanksgiving, sad tears, endurance for temporary annoyance, forgiveness of our neighbour, knowledge of spiritual law and the existence of the justice of God. Thus a person must long for silence if they desire all these spiritual treasures!"

SPIRITUAL READINGS

There is a close relationship between spiritual readings and prayer for "Reading is the fountain of pure prayer." Spiritual readings assist in correcting prayer, thus St Paul advised his disciple Timothy to "give attention to reading." (1 Tim 4:13) Spiritual reading is divided into two sections: reading the Books of the Holy Bible, and reading spiritual books in general.

The life of our Lord Jesus gave us an idea of the importance of the Word in our life. He taught us to memorise the Word of God in our hearts and use it in our struggle against our enemies, as the Lord used it in His temptations on the mountain and as He faced the Cross. St Eronimus advised his disciple Yostikhium saying, "Do not sleep without holding the Bible in your hand to read and if you do sleep and your face falls, let it fall on the Holy Bible."

St Isaac teaches us the importance of spiritual readings in our prayers. He writes based on his own experiences.

• Thoughts are gathered from reading, but we acquire chastity and purity only through prayer.

• Reading makes the inner person a new creation. Prayer energises one's spirit, making the mind ascend above all earthly interests.

• When you read spiritual books, your mind will concentrate and return to more focused prayer.

• Through reading, the mind is open to understanding and this understanding assists in the passion of prayer.

• If one attaches themselves to reading and prayer, they are strengthened and are able to rise above all devilish traps.

• When your thoughts begin to scatter, focus on reading more than prayer.

• If possible, concentrate on reading for it is the source of pure prayer.

• Constant reading, silence and prayer strengthens

the soul.

• Fervent prayers with constant selective reading, will help our mind feel the presence of God.

STRUGGLE AND FORCING

Bishop Agathon was once asked, "Which virtue is better than struggle?" He replied, "Nothing is greater than the struggle of praying constantly to God. When a person tries to pray all the time, the devils try to prevent him. Although the struggle is hard, the soul receives rest from prayer."

St Marcos the great says, "Whoever prays constantly, needs to struggle alot for the evil one will attack him and bring the desire of sleep, laziness, tiredness of the body, boredom, various thoughts and many tricks to stop him praying. Thus, prayer involves a struggle as the devil is always wanting to snatch the soul from God."

St Nilus the Sinai says, "Every war between us and the evil spirits is a result of spiritual prayer. Prayer is a destructive spiritual weapon that can be used against the devils."

The saints show us the nature of prayer and the struggles that accompany it. Prayer requires much struggle, but it also reaps much blessing. The way of worship is hard and the Lord Jesus described it as a narrow gate and a difficult passage. St Paul emphasises this, "For we do not wrestle against flesh and blood, but against principalities, against powers, against the rulers of the darkness of this age, against spiritual hosts of wickedness in the heavenly places...praying always with all prayer and supplication in the Spirit, being watchful to this end with all perseverance and supplication for all the saint." (Eph 6:12, 18)

There is an important principle in the spiritual life that the fathers call the principle of coercion. In life we do not gain anything except by struggle and hard work. A student, a merchant or a farmer do not get what they want if they do not struggle and work hard; similarly we are not worthy of the kingdom of God unless we struggle. Our Lord Jesus Christ showed us the struggle of prayer as He spent whole nights in prayer. His prayers in Gethsemane turned his sweat into drops of blood. We read a lot about the struggle of saints in prayer and the many blessings they became worthy of...

Some of St Isaac's sayings about the struggle of prayer and its blessings:

• Forcing oneself is very important in prayer, in reading the Bible and in attending various services in the church. Do not obey the lazy body that is full of sin as the body always wants to rest.

• Every prayer that does not tire the body and sadden the heart, is like a premature baby born dead.

• If prayer was only linked to struggle, a person cannot continue but, thanks to God, the more we struggle, the more heavenly support we receive.

St Isaac has many experiences in this matter. He says:

• As much as a person struggles and forces himself for the sake of God, as much godly support surrounds him to facilitate his struggle and clear the way before him. If someone asks to what extent I should force myself, I say force yourself for the sake of God, until death. It is better for us to die in struggle than to live in failure.

• If you come out of prayer without fruit and remember nothing of it, then know that there is darkness within you and its remedy is more prayer. However, if a person struggles and is steadfast in his prayers, he will feel the presence and the support of God in everything he does.

• Meditate on the good things that are obtained through struggle. When a person bends his knees in prayer, lifts his hands to heaven and raises his face to the cross, his movements and thoughts are concentrated on God. His heart will be moved and his spirit will be full of Joy.

• If you do not struggle, you will not find. If you do not knock on the door constantly, you will not be heard. Be patient in the darkness of pain, continue your spiritual readings, persevere on forced prayers and you will receive the Grace of God without knowing.

• As much as a person struggles for the sake of God, as much as his heart will have an influence on his prayers.

• Forced prayers presented in humbleness, will always yield a Grace full of comfort and rest.

• If one does not feel the support of his prayers, he should not complain or give up. A farmer does not expect fruit from the moment he plants seeds in the ground. But after many struggles, the farmer enjoys the fruit of his work.

The struggle in prayer is hard as we said, but the

believer turns to it because of all the blessings associated with it. Forced struggle will not always required force. Whatever you do by force and struggle now, you will do by comfort and joy later. St Makarius the Great says: "A person who wishes to come to God must continue praying and force himself to be humble. Whatever he forces himself in today, will be done in Joy and acceptance later. Thus, one trains himself in the life of righteousness and loving God."

DELAY IN ANSWERING PRAYER

It is beneficial to understand all the promises of God and not take some and leave some, otherwise we will start doubting and feeling weak. An example is a person who concentrates on the promises of God in answering prayers and does not realise that there is a valid reason behind the delay of his prayer. Consequently, this individual may become sad, depressed and doubtful. Let us feel the fatherhood of God. Out of His love and wisdom, He will only give good gifts. We should feel that whatever comes to us is for our good as it is coming from "The Beneficent." St John Chrysostom says, "Prayer is a great blessing if it is practised with proper inner feelings. We must give thanks to God whether we receive or not receive our request. For God when He gives or does not give is doing what is good for us. So if you receive what you asked for, it is good, and if you do not receive what you ask for, it is also good for God is always giving what is good for us, and we should trust Him in that."

There are many reasons for delayed answered prayers, as mentioned by St Isaac:

• If God delayed when you asked, do not be saddened, for you are not wiser than God. This is because either your work was not sufficient for asking, or your heart was away from your prayer. The Lord may delay answering for a wisdom He sees. For example, Zacharias and Elizabeth and their prayers to have children. Though they were righteous before God (Lk 1:6), the Lord postponed answering their prayer until they were graced by the birth of John the Baptist who was given the title of "The greatest of those born of women."

• St Basil the Great tells us that if we do receive a prayer request quickly, we will not feel its value and consequently, lose it quickly. However, that which we labour and struggle for, we tend to care for more. St Isaac says, "It is not proper that precious and great things come easily to us, lest the gift of God is not appreciated. Everything that comes quickly goes quickly too while everything that comes with difficulty will be taken care of cautiously."

• Our requests may not be for our own good, thus we do not receive it from God, the Lover of mankind. St Isaac says, "Not every desire that seems good is of benefit. This desire may be from the devil so we must continue praying to ascertain the benefit of this desire."

• The love of God may delay responding to our prayers so that we may pray more and ask earnestly. St Isaac says, "The Lord may give His servant a feeling of weakness, so that this servant may come closer to God, continue knocking and continue asking. Consequently, this servant spends more time talking to God and pleading to Him. Once the prayer request is granted, the servant may no longer ask, therefore become lazy and lukewarm."

St Isaac says, "We learn from the righteous Daniel, who started praying from day one, but only received an answer to his prayer after twenty one days. The angel said to Daniel: "Do not fear, Daniel, for from the first day that you set your heart to understand, and to humble yourself before your God, your words were heard; and I have come because of your words." (Daniel 10:12)

We should not be slack in our prayers for our request may be delayed according to the wisdom of God. We cannot receive the Grace of God if we became lazy or slack in asking. It could have happened to Daniel if he did not continue praying for 21 days.

St Isaac clarified the secret behind the delay in answering prayers by saying, "God, the Master of all, does not look at our requests as an extension to His abundant blessings, and if we thought so, then we are sinful. However, our continuous requests and our sad conscience will enlighten us and give us support in all necessary matters."

HOW TO PRAY

THE POSITION OF THE BODY AND PRAYER

The position of the body during prayer has an effect on the alertness of thoughts. A person is not only a spirit but a body and a spirit and both affect each other. In addition, the position of the body during prayer indicates our respect, fear and supplication before the Lord, which results in the answering of our prayers and the receiving of blessings and spiritual gifts.

St Isaac explains this matter and calls it "The proper attire in prayer." He says, "According to what a person shows in prayer by his body and conscience, there is purity and enlightenment in prayer that enables him to receive many blessings from above."

• A person will quickly be ready for the work of the Holy Spirit when they spread their hands to heaven and bow their face to the ground.

• My brothers, learn that when we do any work for the sake of God, God watches the proper attire we appear in as this implies our respect and attention to Him. None of this is for His benefit, but for our benefit and our salvation.

• Many believe that it is enough to pray with the heart, as God does not want anything else. Therefore, they think it fine to pray while sleeping or sitting, without showing respect with our body in the way we lift our hands and bow our heads. This is an attack from the enemy.

Showing respect by standing up, bowing or lifting the hands is not mandatory for everyone, as the sick and the weak have special orders. St Isaac says, "God is merciful, loving and righteous. He will not judge when one cannot perform what is necessary but will judge on things that can be done but are neglected." He also says, "Whatever we do, we need to do in fear, awe and respect. God in His mercy accepts the little things done with a good intention for He knows our weak nature before He created us."

We should also mention here the tricks of the devil when the children of God intend to pray. As previously mentioned, the weak and sick have their own order in the struggles of prayer, but from experience and the sayings of the fathers we know that both the body and the devil have their tricks. The body is against the spirit and wants only rest. A person may feel weak physically and suffer a headache when he intends to pray. This may be a trick from the lazy body or a war from the devil.

There is an expressive story in the Paradise of the Holy Fathers about a monk who whenever he intended to pray felt feverish and much pain in his head. So he would say to himself, "You wicked one, maybe you will die this hour, pray before you die." Thus, he would finish his prayers and as soon as this happened, the fever and pains would stop. He suffered from this war for sometime but he discovered the trick of the enemy and continued being honest in his prayers until the Lord took away this war from him.

Thus we must be careful if we feel tired and distinguish its kind by talking to our spiritual fathers and consulting the lives of the saints.

There are many positions for the body in prayer. Not everybody will follow the same one but the person praying will use the position that fits with his feelings at the time of prayer.

• Standing in prayer is the common position. The Lord Jesus said, "And whenever you stand praying, if you have anything against anyone, forgive him..." (Mark 11:25); This is accompanied by lifting up the hands. David the prophet says, "Hear the voice of my supplications when I cry to You, when I lift up my hands toward Your holy sanctuary." (Psalm 28:2); and St Paul says, "I desire therefore that the men pray everywhere, lifting up holy hands, without wrath and doubting." (1 Tim 2:8)

• As for kneeling or bowing, this suits the time of confession of sins before God. St Paul says, "For this reason I bow my knees to the Father of our Lord Jesus Christ, from whom the whole family in heaven and earth is named," (Eph 3:14,15) and the Psalmist says, "Oh come, let us worship and bow down; Let us kneel before the LORD our Maker." (Psalm 95:6) Our Lord Jesus Himself bowed on His knees and prayed in Gethsemane. (Luke 22:41)

• The praying person can lower his face to the ground. The Bible mentions Moses and Aaron, and how "they fell on their faces, and said, "O God, the God of the spirits of all flesh, shall one man sin, and You be angry with all the congregation?" (Num 16:22) Jesus Christ Himself, "fell on His face, and prayed" in the garden of Gethsemane. (Matt 26:39)

Raising the eyes to God in prayer has a very important value and effect, even if the eyes are closed. David the

Prophet says, "Unto You I lift up my eyes, O You who dwell in the heavens." (Psalm 123:1) He also says, "To You, O LORD, I lift up my soul." (Psalm 25:1) Stop thinking of earthly things and lift your eyes to heaven, thinking of God alone. These eyes cannot be disappointed, "Turn your eyes away from me, for they have overcome me." (Song of Songs 6:5)

PREPARATION FOR PRAYER

A person needs a period to prepare himself for prayer. This preparation period is necessary whether in the morning when the spirit is heavy from sleep; or at the end of the day with all that took place. St Isaac says, "Before going before Him in prayer, prepare yourself as necessary." Calm yourself a little before starting prayer as you need to prepare yourself emotionally. It is not proper to move from what you were doing to prayer right away for if you did that, you will not enjoy prayer and your thoughts will be scattered in whatever you were just involved in. John Cassaian says, "No matter what thoughts we had before prayer, these will recur during prayer through our memory, thus, we should prepare ourselves for prayer beforehand. During prayer, the mind recalls previous events, words, or thoughts which may result in the arousal of our anger, laughter or certain lusts. Therefore, if we do not want any of those to come during our prayers, we must expel these matters from our hearts, before we set off with prayer."

During this short preparation period, around five to ten minutes, according to your own circumstances, try to increase your spiritual zeal by reading a part of the Holy Bible for comfort, rather than for study. This means, do not indulge in questions that can be postponed to the time you study the Bible. In addition, you may praise the Lord, sing a hymn, or just contemplate on one of the characteristics of God like His love to mankind and His abundant blessings. You can use this preparation time to think of your sins, and count how many times you angered the Lord. A person cannot really follow one way for he is not always at the same spiritual level. Sometimes he is happy and prefers singing, other times he is comforted so silence suits him. Yet, other times he may feel despaired, so thinking about God's mercy is most needed.

There is also another feeling that you need to fill your heart with before prayer. Feel that you are standing before God and that He hears you, sees you and is so close to you, for this will fill you with hope. Before lifting your hands, lift your soul and say with David "I lift up my soul to You Lord." Before lifting your eyes, lift up your heart. There is also another advice that St Isaac says, "Before starting your prayer, cross your heart and your body by the sign of the Cross. Stand still for a minute until your senses relax and your movement quietens; then lift your inner sight to God asking Him to strengthen your weakness by His Grace." It is also good to prepare yourself for prayer by bowing several times and asking for God's mercy.

CONTROLLING THOUGHTS DURING PRAYER

"These people draw near to Me with their mouth, and honor Me with their lips, but their heart is far from Me." (Matt 15:8) These are the words that our Lord Jesus said when he scolded the scribes and Pharisees. It clarifies an important principle in prayer: the prayer of the lips is not what is required. God longs for the prayer of the heart. When you pray, struggle to control your thoughts and let them follow with what your heart is saying. St John El Tabysy says, "If you say a written prayer, do not just read it, but make its words your words so that your prayer comes from the heart." He also says, "Do not think, my brother that prayer is just words that you can learn. You are talking to a Spiritual God, so your prayer needs to be spiritual, not merely words spoken or read. Therefore, the mind and heart must participate with the tongue in prayer; the mind realises what is said, the heart feels what the mind is thinking, and the lips utter words of the spirit. Many times, the tongue is saying holy prayer while the heart is not feeling its meaning at all. Real prayer is where the thoughts are united by the feelings of the heart.

In order to control one's thoughts during prayer, one must not occupy their thoughts with any other matter. The Lord Jesus said, "When you pray, go into your room, and when you have shut your door..." (Matt 6:6) this means, do not occupy your mind with many matters for the room of the spirit is the body and its doors are the five bodily senses. The senses are the entry of knowledge, so we should close all these windows so nothing can come in and disturb our thoughts during prayer. St Evagrius says, "Ignore the needs of the body when you stand for prayer. Even if you are bitten by a fly or an insect, do not be bothered by it so as not to lose the great benefit of prayer."

Saints Nilus El Sinai and Evagrius tell us an impressive story about how we should not occupy our minds with anything, during prayer. Once there was a brother walking in the wilderness praying, and two angels appeared to him and walked beside him. One angel was on his right and the other on his left. The brother did not look at either of them so that he may not lose the fruit of prayer. He reminded himself of the sayings of St Paul: "No angels, archangels, or principalities can separate us from the love of Jesus..." The stories of the fathers of the wilderness are full of similar examples. They would not stop praying even if the devil appeared to them in forms of animals and dangerous serpents.

WANDERING THOUGHTS IN PRAYER

This is the term used by the saints, which means unconcentrated thoughts in prayer. It is seldom known that a person can concentrate totally on one subject for a long time, whether it is reading, studying, discussion or prayer. After long struggles, few of the fathers were able to conquer this by "crucifying their mind." A person who is attached to certain lusts will certainly have a wandering mind; while the person who is full with many foods, will find it difficult to control or direct his thoughts. Jesus mentioned this when He said, "But take heed to yourselves, lest your hearts be weighed down with carousing, drunkenness, and cares of this life." (Luke 21:34) St Isaac says, "Do not fill your stomach lest your mind wander and you cannot be in control when you stand to pray; you will be lazy and relaxed and will not be fair to yourself. You will be unable to gather your words and even the Psalms will not be pleasant to you."

It is impossible for us to stop wandering thoughts for we are still beginners in the spiritual life. However the saints differentiated between two kinds of wandering.

Sometimes our thoughts may wander into spiritual matters, while other times our thoughts may wander into matters, not suitable for prayer. There is both good and bad wandering. Dear brother, do not wait until you have a non-wandering conscience for this is impossible, but let your thoughts wander on spiritual matters.

Therefore, if the wandering of thoughts is unavoidable, then God is not angry from us except if we listen to it and not resist it. St Isaac says, "We are not judged when there are thoughts within us but we find Grace if we resist it. We are judged if we agree to it."

St Isaac says, "Pure prayer is not without wandering thoughts but is when the mind wanders in useful and righteous matters acceptable by God." Also he says, "Evil wandering is when a person thinks wrong thoughts during his prayer before God, but the correct wandering is when he thinks about the glory of God, as these thoughts help in the purity of prayer and the gathering of thoughts." St Isaac even goes further saying, "It is very proper to gather the mind to think about heavenly matters. This wandering is better than pure prayer."

Some people get too annoyed about the negative wandering of their thoughts as they see it as disrespect to God, so they stop praying. However, in order to treat bad wandering thoughts, one must pray more, read more on spiritual matters, practice seclusion, struggle against it and fear God.

Regarding this, St Isaac says:

• Do not wait for your wandering thoughts to stop in order to pray. Instead battle off all wandering thoughts with continuous prayer.

• Nothing can control the mind and save from sins, more than repeating the name of God.

• Always mix prayer with spiritual reading. This will gather the thoughts and help the mind focus on spiritual things.

• One cannot have clear vision while standing beside smoke. Similarly, the heart cannot obtain purity and silence of thoughts unless they hide themselves from the smoke of the "world" which obscures the eyes of the spirit.

• In order to stop wandering thoughts, protect yourself from the desires of your senses and any materialistic lust.

• Where the fear of God is, there is pure prayer without wandering.

• A person is expected to receive wandering thoughts while praying, but he is not expected to pay attention to them.

• Singing hymns is a cure for wandering thoughts.

THE WARMTH OF PRAYER

Controlling our mind against wandering thoughts will allow us to reach the state of pure, undefiled prayer. This pure prayer produces spiritual warmth which David mentions in his Psalm, "My heart was hot within me; while I was musing, the fire burned. Then I spoke with my tongue." (Psalm 39:3) This is a special spiritual fire which our Lord kindles in each one of our hearts. He says, "I came to send fire on the earth, and how I wish it were already kindled!"

(Luke 12:49) This is the fire that burned in the heart of Cleopas and his companion when they cried joyfully, "Did not our heart burn within us while He talked with us on the road, and while He opened the Scriptures to us." (Luke 24:32) St Isaac says, "Strong work produces warmth in the heart. This warmth is given through meditation and tears. Constant tears calms the thoughts and cleanses the mind, allowing the soul to see spiritual visions and hear spiritual secrets."

THE SPEECH OF PRAYER

Let your prayer be simple with God, without decorative language. It is a dialogue between a son and His heavenly Father. It is dialogue between a lover and His Beloved!! St Augustine says, "At the start of your prayer, say Our Father who art in heaven... This call will make your heart move with love, for there is nothing more precious than the love of a Father to his child. This is the Grace of Sonship!!"

Do not think that prayer is made up of a few phrases, coupled with some memorised verses and prepared words. Real prayer is a natural conversation; do not be obliged to use classical language that may hinder you from an easy dialogue with your Loved One. God understands all languages and accents, then do not be too formal in your prayers for our relationship with God is that of sons and not slaves. He did not give us a bondage spirit of fear but sonship so that we can cry 'Our Abba Father.'

You are alone before Him so be free from yourself and the ties of society and talk to Him about your troubles, pains, love and longings. Tell Him "I am defeated in such and such and I long to live for You in purity and righteousness. Please strengthen me and help me." Have a conversation and discussion with God like David, "If You, LORD, should mark iniquities, O Lord, who could stand?" Remind Him of His mercies and His benefits towards the fathers of past generations and ask Him to treat you the same, for He is the same yesterday, today, forever.

We advise you to use the singular noun in your prayer. Do not say, "We are sinners and often upset You and do not follow Your commandments," but say "I am a sinner and I often upset You and do not follow Your commandments." Do not say, "The world and its lust is fighting us and many times we have fallen," but say, "The world and its lust is fighting me, My Lord, and I have fallen many times." Singular expressions will put you face to face before God and will help you converse with God on a personal level.

We see this clearly in the Gregory Liturgy, which is full of expressive phrases. Although it is used in church and prayed on behalf of everybody, St Gregory the Theologian preferred to write it as a meditative conversation with the Son of God. For example, he says, "You, as a Lover of mankind, created me, a man. You had no need of my servitude; rather it was me who was in need of Your lordship. Because of the multitude of Your compassions, You formed me when I had no being. For my sake You bridled the sea. For my sake You have revealed the nature of the animals. You subdued everything under my feet. You wrote within me the image of Your authority; and placed within me the gift of speech. You opened for me the paradise, for my delight; and gave me the learning of Your knowledge. You, O my Master have turned for me punishment into salvation. You are He who sent to me the prophets, for my sake, I the sick. You gave me the Law as an aid. You are He Who ministered to me salvation when I transgressed Your Law." How wonderful these phrases as they ascend the spirit and make the soul long for heavenly matters.

ASPECTS OF PRAYER

Prayer is not just a list of requests we ask from God, otherwise it would be a take relationship only. Our requests are not supposed to be about ourselves only. We should make requests for others as this is love and service. Requests may be for the salvation of others or for their physical healing. There are other aspects that should be included in our prayer as expressed in the Apostle's words, "Therefore I exhort first of all that supplications, prayers, intercessions, and giving of thanks be made for all men." (1 Tim 2:1) St Basil the Great and Origen mentioned four aspects to consider in our prayers:

• Glorify God with all our strength and ability, as expressed in Psalms 103 and 104.

• Thank God for all His goodness towards mankind as in David's thanksgiving prayer in 2 Samuel chapter 22.

• Confess past sins and plead for forgiveness and healing of all spiritual disease.

• Prayer for other people

• Prayer for your own spiritual, psychological or physical needs.

SOME PROBLEMS OF PRAYER

PRAYER WHICH IS LUKEWARM

This is where a person does not desire to pray because he does not feel any comfort in prayer. He does not feel relaxed and is always wanting to end his prayer quickly. He feels that his prayers do not pass his lips and this is called, "drought in prayer."

This lukewarm state may be caused by us or the devil. We can cause ourselves to grow lukewarm if we are attached to certain worldly lusts or if we suffer physically or mentally from weak health, lack of physical fitness or pressure that leads to laziness of the mind. We can also feel lukewarm as a result of the devil. The devil will attack us with boredom, carelessness and wandering thoughts, which prevent the comfort of prayer. However, sometimes God prevents His comfort as a test of our love and faith or because He knows it will benefit us spiritually.

If our lukewarm state in praying is a result of a certain lust of the heart, this must be treated by repentance. If this is a result of exhaustion then we need to change the time of prayer to when the body is rested and energetic. Thus the early hours of the day are the most suitable for prayer. There is a common error that many fall into which is praying at night after being tired from the day's work. Surely, they will not feel the comforts of prayer.

If our lukewarm state is an attack from the devil, we can conquer him by perseverance and struggle. We should know that the comforts of prayer are a gift from God to the beginners in their spiritual struggle, but we cannot depend on these comforts in our spiritual wars. A soldier is sent to war with military music to encourage him but this does not continue in the battle! It is an encouragement for the first push. It is the same with our spiritual struggle.

Those stuck in the lukewarm state will suffer doubt. They will examine themselves and find that they are regular in their spiritual practices yet still, they feel lukewarm. This is where the devil interferes and makes them think that they are failures in their spiritual life and that the Lord is not near them so they are not comforted or at peace. However, this may be according to God's wisdom to protect us from haughtiness from the many comforts in prayer.

As a remedy for this lukewarm state, steadfastness is needed even if God seems far away. The cure is to continue praying and not to give in to this state. We should continue looking towards God even if we do not see Him. Moreover, we should not depend on feelings in our relationship with God. The comforts of prayer are like smiles of approval. A son needs these smiles from his father. However, if God does not smile in our faces one day, this does not mean we lost our sonship!

The Lord may prevent us from the comforts of prayer to educate us for our practice. If we are constantly comforted, we may think ourselves saints and fall into pride. The Lord gives us gifts and helps us protect these gifts from pride. If God prevents us from His comforts, this does not mean that He is upset from us. When a mother teaches her child to walk, she does not always hold his hand, so that the child may fall, cry and yearn for his mother's hand again. This is just like the Grace of God. It may leave us for a little while, causing us to feel a need and cry to God again. The prayers we pray while in spiritual drought are still accepted before God. On the contrary, the Lord accepts these prayers more than the prayers of comfort because the value of prayers is not measured by the comfort it brings but by the degree of struggle.

Many Psalms express spiritual drought in prayer, such as Psalms 10, 13, 22, 88, 102, 130 and 140. For example, in Psalm 13, David says: "How long, O LORD? Will You forget me forever? How long will You hide Your face from me?" However, at the end of the Psalm he prays, "But I have trusted in Your mercy; my heart shall rejoice in Your salvation. I will sing to the LORD, because He has dealt bountifully with me." In the beginning of Psalm 22, David says, "My God, My God, why have You forsaken Me...O My God, I cry in the daytime, but You do not hear; and in the night season, and am not silent." Towards the end of the Psalm he says, "I will declare Your name to My brethren; in the midst of the assembly I will praise You. You who fear the LORD, praise Him! All you descendants of Jacob, glorify Him... For He has not despised nor abhorred the affliction of the afflicted; nor has He hidden His face from Him; but when He cried to Him, He heard."

A person is mistaken if he expects joy always in his prayers and is upset when he does not feel this. Our goal in the spiritual life is not gladness but joy of the Lord Himself. During times of spiritual drought, we must go to the Lord in prayer and carry it as a cross to Jesus. We must ask ourselves clearly and honestly, 'What is the aim and goal of our spiritual struggle? Is it to feel comfortable and glad or is it to be close to God?'

THE PROBLEM OF TIME

People are busy with their work and responsibilities so they cannot find time for prayer. These people need to practise time management so as to fulfil their duties towards God. One should avoid wasting time in socialising and wasteful discussions. Prayer is very important and time should be set for it daily.

The seven prayers of the Agbia are not only set for monks, but are set for the whole congregation. The seven prayers are mentioned in the laws of Nicaea's Council of 325AD, but were also mentioned during the apostles' time and in the laws of the beginning of the third century A.D. Prayer adds blessing to our lives so we must never make excuses to avoid it. We will be blamed before our conscience if we prefer a minor task over prayer for prayer nourishes our spiritual life and strengthens our relationship with God and people. We do not deny that some people are pressured with so many obligations. Although they intend to lengthen their times of prayer, they fail due to their many responsibilities. In this case, they are not blamed because God can see their good intentions for prayer yet their multiple circumstances. Their intention to pray is pure and acceptable before the Lord.

There are other people who do not pray sufficiently. They blame it on their lack of time, while they are actually careless in setting strict times for prayer. These people avoid prayer because they do not feel its benefit and they believe that the psalms are for monks and priests.

As a remedy for this, a person must be convinced of the importance of prayer, thus, spend effort in setting necessary time for it. He should set a short program that he can fulfil if his time will not allow him to pray all the prayers. Whatever the duties are, most people set time for prayer in the early morning and in the evening. The one who starts his day with God, continues his day properly by the help of His Grace. In regards to the Agbia prayer before sleep, it is preferred to pray it before dinner or in the evening, because one gets exhausted if it is left to the late night. Just before sleeping, one may pray any personal prayer from his heart so as to give oneself to God and plead for protection throughout the night.

During the day, we advise that a person pray to God in his heart in any way. It is important to memorise the psalms so that they may be recalled throughout the day. He can pray while on the road or during his work, whether standing, sitting or walking.

For example, if God gave a person some free time at noon and he is able to pray all the prayers of the sixth hour, he should thank God from all his heart. If he only has a few minutes, he can pray the Gospel and the following parts which will be enough. If he does not have time at all, he can pray a part like "Lord Jesus, on the sixth day ..." The important thing is that one does not leave the occasion without praying and being blessed by it. In this way, we remember the Lord in every hour of our day.

PROBLEM OF FINDING A PLACE FOR PRAYER

Due to the increase in population, the smaller area for buildings and the high rental values, families now live in smaller units where one may not find place to pray. Two siblings may be sharing a room, so each sibling does not have an isolated place for their individual prayers. If the family is not spiritual, one may not be able to pray comfortably in their house. Praying in the presence of another person who is not praying, may be uncomfortable but one must keep steadfast in his prayer and this may win others to Jesus. I knew a young student in military college who used to stand beside his bed and pray the Psalms, among all his colleagues, without any embarrassment. When the supervisors knew about this, they respected him more. Some people may wake up earlier than the rest of the family or stay up at night until all the family is asleep, to overcome this problem. We do not deny that this is difficult but it is a kind of struggle that has its crown and reward.

Families seldom allocate a place for prayer, like a corner of prayer. It would be great if every family payed attention to this and allocated a certain place in the house for prayer. This place can be decorated with icons and candles. There are many blessings in doing this as it spreads the prayer atmosphere in the house. We should pay attention to this corner of our house more than any other because this is where the family meets the Lord and lays all their troubles before Him.

THE PROBLEM OF EMBARRASSMENT

Some people get embarrassed to pray in front of others, even if it is their family members. If a person is affected by this, he should train himself gradually to overcome it by concentrating on his prayers to God while not paying attention to people. Also include a special prayer for this problem.

THE SECRECY IN PRAYER

Praying in secret is a commandment of Jesus to all the faithful. (Matt 6:6) But some misunderstand this commandment and go further away from what the Lord means. When the Lord Jesus commanded us to pray in secrecy, He did not mean that nobody should see us or that no one should know that we pray, but he meant for us to avoid hypocrisy, showing off and wanting the glory of people. In whatever we do, whether prayer or deed, the Lord Jesus commanded us to do so from the heart for Him only. If He meant that no one sees us at all when we pray, then how can we explain His saying, "Let your light so shine before men, that they may see your good works and glorify your Father in heaven." (Matt 5:16). The devil fights some people with these ideas to stop them from praying if someone enters the room, etc.

ANNOYANCE FROM THE FAMILY

This point affects mainly youth and children who come from unspiritual families. The family may make fun of the youth who prays by convincing them that they are wrong. The family may prevent them from going to spiritual meetings or interfere with their freedom. The family may open the television loudly when they know the youth is trying to pray. However, the steadfastness of the youth against these annoyances will be blessed by God. It may also lead the rest of the family to God at one point or another.

CONSTANT PRAYER

High levels of prayer can be reached by people living in the world, just as much as it is reached by those living in the wilderness. Despite all worldly activities and duties, high levels of prayer can be attained if one utilises all chances available. St Paul advises the believers to "pray without ceasing." Although David was a King with many responsibilities, he would say, "Seven times every day, I will praise your name," and "At midnight I will rise to give thanks to you." What does this mean? Should a person stop working to fulfil the commandment "pray without ceasing?" Of course not...

However, it is possible to combine work with prayer? The state of continuance prayer is derived from love. For example, we can say that a man loves his wife and is always thinking of her. This does not mean he stops working to think of his wife all the time. His mind is busy with work, but at the same time, his heart is full of love towards his wife. Similarly, is the life of love with God as it leads us to think of Him continually and thus, pray without ceasing.

Prayer does not only consist of thoughts and words but also actions. St Klemandus the Alexandrian says that all intellectual works are considered different deeds of prayer.

FEELING THE PRESENCE OF GOD

The more I talk to God, the more I feel His presence with me. If we are close to a certain person, we miss them when they leave us. Feeling the presence of God is like feeling the presence of a dear friend. The only difference is that we can see our friend in sight, while we can only feel God's presence in spirit. The Lord dwells in our hearts. He waits for us there and whispers and speaks. If we want to feel the presence of God, we must look inside our hearts. St Augustine realised this by saying, "I loved You very late, the very Old Beauty, though new." Then he cries saying, "I loved You very late!! For You were inside me and I was outside searching for You in a different way."

SHORT REPETITIVE PRAYERS

Because the soul feels the love of God inside her, the spirit expresses her love, joy and needs in short repetitive prayers that do not need concentration or effort. These prayers do not need a certain time, place or atmosphere for it is the conversation of man to the Almighty Who lives within. We can express our feelings in these short prayers while on the road, on a bus, alone or with people. In general, we can pray anywhere and in every occasion. There are beautiful words sung in the Saturday praises: "With every breath I bless Your Holy Name." Yes every breath blesses You my Lord and praises You my Beloved. Carry my feelings of love as my heart longs to be with You always...

Always feel that the Lord is with you. Train yourself in this. For when you have this feeling, you will cry with the bride, "When I found the one I love, I held him and would not let him go." (Song of Songs 3:4) This exercise needs training and patience. In the beginning, it will need effort and forcing, but as you practice it, you will be able to feel God's presence without any effort on your side.

EXAMPLES

• The prayer of the Lord Jesus Christ: The faithful will repeat the name of Jesus accompanied with a short prayer like, 'My Lord Jesus Christ the Son of God have mercy on me'... 'My Lord Jesus Christ help me'... 'My Lord Jesus Christ take away this evil thought from me'... 'My Lord Jesus Christ calm down my body'... 'My Lord Jesus Christ stop all evil forces'... 'Teach me to love you My Lord Jesus Christ'... and so on. This prayer has been used since the old ages. There are references to it in the writings of St Ephraim, John Chrysostom, Parsnofious and John El Daragy. This prayer needs love and perseverance. It is a short prayer but it keeps the heart holy and in constant communication with the Creator. The name of the Lord is strong and effective and it is salvation to those who call on Him, "The name of the LORD is a strong tower; the righteous run to it and are safe." (Prov 18:10) The name of the Lord frightens the devil, "But Paul, greatly annoyed, turned and said to the spirit, "I command you in the name of Jesus Christ to come out of her." (Acts 16:18) If you are attacked by devilish thoughts or if you are subject to bad habits, we suggest these prayers as they are powerful.

• Praying Psalm 69: "Make haste, O God, to deliver me! Make haste to help me, O LORD!" All the monks in Egypt rely on the power of this prayer. John Cassian talks about his experiences with this psalm: "This is a call to God in danger and a humble confession. This phrase is a protective fence against all the devil's attacks, as well as a shield that cannot be penetrated. This expression is useful to everyone in all circumstances. Repeat it at all times. Putting this psalm in your heart will not only protect you from the devil's attacks but will cleanse you from earthy sins. Sleep while you are repeating it. When you wake up, let it be the first thing you think of."

PRAYER ACCORDING TO A DISCIPLINE

IS IT BETTER TO HAVE A CERTAIN RULE FOR WORSHIP?

A written prayer can become automatic and routine-like. Sometimes we say the written prayer with our tongues while our hearts are inclined far. On the other hand, if we do not have a specific discipline in our prayers, we will pray only when we feel like it and this is dangerous. We will grow up not caring about prayer and irregular prayers will probably end up into no prayer at all.

A disciplined prayer is not an insult to God. What matters to God are two things: First, that our will moves towards Him and second, that there is a reason for our actions. To have a specific discipline in prayer shows God our perseverance to pray regularly regardless of current conditions. The set rule of prayer is like a contract that a person must follow in honesty. It is clear that engaging ourselves with such a discipline is an act of long term will power. It is better than leaving ourselves to pray whenever we feel a need for such a need will eventually go away.

Our attachment to a discipline in prayer is a support for us. Many times we may need a push to pray and a discipline in prayer achieves this. Prayer is not only a relationship with God but it is a struggle against our spiritual enemies. Our attachment to a discipline in prayer assists us to cross over these difficulties.

The saintly fathers had a discipline for worship set up by the elderly fathers. This discipline helped them start up their spiritual lives and resist the devil. St Eronimus said says: "It is important to specify a certain time for prayer so that if we are occupied at this time, it will remind us of our duty." There is nothing wrong with organised worship but it is wrong to carry it in an automatic way that will make it lose its effect and worth.

PRAYING THE PSALMS

Why did the church choose the Psalms of David the Prophet and organise them into an Agbia? I do not want to answer this question with my own words but I want you to hear what St John Chrysostom says, "We read the Books of the Old Testament once a year with an effort; we read the Holy Gospels and the Epistles once or twice a week at church. However, the Holy Spirit prepared the Agbia on the Psalms of David to encourage prayer in the morning and night. These Psalms are read at the beginning of masses, in spiritual meetings and funerals. The church even encourages his members to memorise these psalms. In all occasions, David's Psalms are available.

The psalms are like angelic praises prepared by God for His servants, thus the earth becomes heaven and humans become angels. David invites sinners to repentance by saying: "Confess to the Lord for He is righteous." He encourages people to give thanks by saying: "How can I reward the Lord for all His benefits?" He calls people to confession by saying, "Have mercy on me Oh Lord, because of Your constant love."

He strengthens those called for priesthood by saying: "Do not cast me away from Your face." He comforts those who are afraid by saying; "Save me Oh God from my enemies." He encourages the patient by saying: "I waited for the Lord and He listened to my request." The Psalms are like a great violin with praises and prayers held in its strings.

The holy church uses the Psalms as a prayer material for the following reasons:

• David had various experiences throughout his life as he was a shepherd, a great prophet and a king. He was a saint and also a man who fell into great sin. Consequently, the Psalms cover a multitude of experiences that will definitely meet our needs.

• David wrote the psalms from a heart that was purified by repentance. He struggled greatly for his spiritual life. "In the day of sorrow, I wore sackcloth and weakened my body with fasting...In the middle of the night I woke up to give thanks for Your righteous judgements... Seven times a day I praise you for Your just judgement...I ate ashes as bread and mixed my drink with my tears." Despite David's strong spiritual life, he fell into sin. So do not be overconfident my brother for "If the righteous will scarcely saved, where will I the sinner appear."

• Although David expressed his thoughts into his psalms, they are actually the Words of God, guided by the Holy Spirit. Therefore, when you pray the Psalms, you are talking to God with His words. When a lawyer is defending a convict, he must address certain parts of the Law to gain credibility. Similarly, when you pray, address the psalms and you will gain mercy and Love from God.

• Our personal prayers are characterised by many requests. However, the psalms teach us to praise our Creator. Praise is the language of heavenly hosts.

• Above all, the Psalms are a great material for meditation for it fills the soul with many beautiful thoughts. The psalms are drenched in the Spirit of God.

• The Psalms are powerful. For this reason, St Isaac says: "May you have an infinite love for the Psalms for they are the food of the spirit."

This does not mean that the prayers of the Psalms are enough. You should also pray private prayers to express your feelings toward God and to ask Him about your needs. The saintly fathers considered the prayer of the Psalms as an introduction to the prayer of the heart.

How do we pray the Psalms?

• Present your prayers in awe and reverence. Raise your hands to heaven in humility and bow humbly. If you are careful in this, St Isaac says: "The Grace of God will visit you, for humility in prayer is very beautiful in the eyes of God." Understand the Psalms and say the words slowly.

• The quality of your prayer matters more than the quantity. St Isaac says, "If you want to enjoy reading the Psalms and tasting the Holy Spirit, do not be bothered about the number of Psalms you pray. It is enough that your mind understands the meanings of the prayer so that you may praise the Lord."

• After every Psalm, make a metania and ask the Lord

one request. If there is a certain habit or sin that you are suffering from, present this weakness before the Lord in every metania you perform. You can also pray for people in this way.

• John Cassain learnt prayer from the monks of the desert. He says, "I saw them in their prayer. After they finish a Psalm, they do not hurry to bow down as an obligation to finish, but I saw them standing for a while and praying a short prayer, then bowing down in awe, with their faces on the ground and then standing again with all thoughts centred in prayer."

• The Kiryelyson (Lord have mercy) that we say during our prayers of the Psalms should be repeated slowly. Every time you say Kiryelyson, imagine the whip that scourged our Lord Jesus. Say within your heart "You did this for me My Lord?" Let the Lord's sufferings encourage you to plead for mercy.

Fasting

∿

"Blow the trumpet in Zion, Consecrate a fast,
Call a sacred assembly;"
(Joel 2: 15)

❧ Spiritual Concept of Fasting

❧ Fasting in the Spiritual life

❧ Why do we fast?

❧ How do we fast?

❧ Advices and guidelines

❧ Fasting in the Coptic Church

SPIRITUAL CONCEPT OF FASTING

Fasting concerns abstaining from food for a period of time, after which vegetarian food can be eaten. According to the saintly fathers, fasting also includes all other forms of asceticism and bodily control. St. John of Tabisse says: "Fasting of the body involves abstinence, and feelings of hunger, but fasting of the soul involves hungering and thirsting after righteousness, as well as fasting from evil tricks of wickedness." St. Paul the Apostle says: "And everyone who competes for the prize is temperate in all thing. But I discipline my body and bring it into subjection, lest, when I have preached to others, I myself should become disqualified." (1 Cor. 9:25)

DISCIPLINING THE BODY

St. Paul the great preacher of the world says: "But I discipline my body and bring it into subjection, lest, when I have preached to others, I myself should become disqualified." Here, we might wonder: would it be possible for this great saint to be disqualified after all of his great work?! After seeing wonderful revelations, would he lose the race?! That is why he says: "I discipline my body and bring it to subjection..." Do not forget that St Paul ascended to the third heaven, saw wonders, and toiled more than any other apostle.

Without a doubt, these words reveal to us the importance of genuine spiritual struggle. The concept of salvation might be unclear to some people, i.e. if someone says 'I am saved' does this mean he/she has already reached heaven and is in no struggle between the body and its desires? It is not possible that a person stops sinning while he/she is alive!! These people have to remember St. Peter's words: "If the righteous one is scarcely saved, Where will the ungodly and the sinner appear?" (1 Peter 4: 18)

Bodily desires and bad habits form a great obstacle in spiritual struggle. Regarding this, St James says: "Where do wars and fights come from among you? Do they not come from your desires for pleasure that war in your members?"(James 4: 1) The Spirit wants to be released to God, while the body is pulling it down to earth. St Paul says: "For the flesh lusts against the Spirit and the Spirit against the flesh; and these are contrary to one another, so that you do not do the things that you wish." (Gal.5: 17)

Furthermore, St. Paul goes on describing that true Christians are the ones who "...have crucified the flesh with its passions and desires." (Gal. 5: 24) Thus, in order to achieve Christian perfection, the discipline of our body should be our priority.

After being put into the fire, Iron is knocked with force in order to give it its final look. Similarly, it is not enough to smooth our hearts with the warmth of prayer, but we also have to knock our spirit with asceticism and austerity, "For if you live according to the flesh, you will die; but if by the Spirit, you put to death the deeds of the body, you will live." (Romans 8: 13)

If we are to follow Christ, we must walk the path of asceticism and austerity; "Always carrying about in the body the dying of the Lord Jesus, that the life of Jesus also may be manifested in our body." (2 Cor. 4: 10)

David the Prophet addresses the Lord saying, "Yet for Your sake we are killed all day long; We are accounted as sheep for the slaughter." (Ps. 44: 22) We do not deserve the real pleasure of the Spirit unless we kill off all bodily and worldly desires. Sarah did this and was able to give birth to a son of the Spirit.

The Lord Jesus didn't go back to His hometown except after the death of Herod who wanted to kill Him. We should be the same, we have to kill Herod who seeks to destroy our soul, "Therefore put to death your members which are on the earth: fornication, uncleanness, passion, evil desire, and covetousness, which is idolatry." (Col. 3: 5) The Lord will not dwell in your heart, unless you overcome your deviated desires and lusts.

Without a doubt, overcoming one's desires and resisting bodily lusts is considered a great struggle, because "He who is slow to anger is better than the mighty, And he who rules his spirit than he who takes a city." (Prov. 16: 32) St Embrose says: "Our desires and bodily lusts are stronger enemies than those in the outer world surrounding us. Resisting Potiphar's wife and her defiled intentions were greater than all the marvellous things which Joseph did in Egypt."

St. John Chrysostom says: "When David overcame his desire to avenge Saul his enemy, this was considered greater than when he killed Goliath. This act was not only announced on earth but in the Heavenly Jerusalem. He made the heavenly hosts rejoice with his victory over his own desire, better than his victory over Goliath."

Fasting helps overcome and discipline the body.

WHAT IS FASTING ?

Fasting is refraining from eating certain kinds of food. A higher spiritual level of fasting is optional asceticism. It is not about making our bodies weak, but it is about disciplining and subjecting our bodies in order to nurture the Spirit. Fasting relates to the Spirit more than the body. Fasting is not atonement for our sins and iniquities, but a preparation of the soul to accept the Lord.

FASTING IN THE SPIRITUAL LIFE

According to the Old and New Testament, fasting has a very special rank in spiritual life. The Lord Jesus honoured fasting through His words and personal practice. Some saints believe that fasting should be ahead of all other struggles in spiritual life as it is fasting which paves the way to all virtues. Unless we discipline and subdue the body, we will be distracted by worldly and bodily lusts which will block our path to heaven.

St. Isaac says: "Struggling against any sin should start with fasting, especially if it is an inner sin." At the beginning of creation, the first commandment was not to eat from the tree of knowledge. This fasting commandment was broken and that was how the first creation fell. Thus, we have to start building by tracing the first fall. Our Lord went into the wilderness, where He fasted for forty days and forty nights. All those who want to follow Christ's footsteps should share in the struggle of fasting.

IN THE OLD TESTAMENT

The first sin of human beings was the failure to fast. God ordered Adam not to eat from a certain tree, but Adam disobeyed, and caused calamity for the entire human race. St. John Chrysostom says: "When God created man, He taught him to discipline his body and acquire salvation through fasting."

"...and the Lord God commanded the man, saying,

"Of every tree of the garden you may freely eat; but of the tree of the knowledge of good and evil you shall not eat, for in the day that you eat of it you shall surely die." Isn't this a kind of fasting? If fasting was so important in Paradise, what about outside Paradise? We heartily need the aid of fasting...

If Adam had listened to God's voice concerning this matter, he wouldn't have heard the order to depart heaven. The Old Testament is full of examples and sayings about fasting. We read about many of the early fathers who fasted and did marvellous works. We also read how congregational fasting attracted God's mercy:

• Moses the Prophet deserved to see God and talk to Him after he fasted forty days. This is when he was handled the Law written by the finger of God.

• Elijah, after fasting for forty days, had the honour of seeing God, giving life to the dead and opening the heavens so that it could rain.

• Esther made the order of destroying her people, void through fasting.

• Daniel was fasting when Archangel Gabriel appeared to him and revealed God's mysteries.

• Judith fasted all her days as a widow. (Judith 8: 5, 6)

• Nehemiah mourned and fasted when he heard the sad news about his brethren in Jerusalem, the destroyed wall and the burnt doors. (Neh 1:4)

• Anna the prophetess, the daughter of Phanuel,

served God with fasting and prayer night and day. (Luke 2 : 37)

• David the Prophet and King gave the best example of continuous fasting by saying, "But as for me, when they were sick, My clothing was sackcloth; I humbled myself with fasting" (Ps. 35: 13) and "My knees are weak through fasting, And my flesh is feeble from lack of fatness." (Ps. 109: 24)

• Ahab the cruel king fasted after hearing Elijah's words; "So it was, when Ahab heard those words, that he tore his clothes and put sackcloth on his body, and fasted and lay in sackcloth, and went about mourning. And the word of the Lord came to Elijah the Tishbite, saying, "See how Ahab has humbled himself before Me? Because he has humbled himself before Me, I will not bring the calamity in his days. In the days of his son I will bring the calamity on his house." (1 Kings 21: 27 – 29)

The Lord talks about acceptable fasting, its conditions and its blessings through Isaiah the Prophet, as seen in Isaiah chapter 58.

A great example of fasting was portrayed by the city of Nineveh and by the Israelites in their war over the tribe of Benjamin. Another great example of fasting was seen by the congregation during the era of Samuel the Prophet. (1 Sam. 7: 6) It is also written in the Holy Bible, "… Jehoshaphat feared, and set himself to seek the Lord, and proclaimed a fast throughout all Judah. So Judah gathered together to ask help from the Lord; and from all the cities of Judah they came to seek the Lord." (2 Chro 20:3)

Ezra called everyone to fast on his way to Jerusalem,

saying "Then I proclaimed a fast there at the river of Ahava, that we might humble ourselves before our God, to seek from Him the right way for us and our little ones and all our possessions. For I was ashamed to request of the king an escort of soldiers and horsemen to help us against the enemy on the road, because we had spoken to the king, saying, "The hand of our God is upon all those for good who seek Him, but His pour and His wrath are against all those who forsake Him."(Ezra 8: 21–23)

IN THE NEW TESTAMENT

Fasting in the Old Testament was not necessarily a resemblance of the New Testament. For example in the Old Testament, animals were burnt as offerings, but this stopped in the New Testament. The Lord Jesus Himself revealed the importance and effectiveness of fasting in the lives of the believers when He fasted for forty days and forty nights. Certainly the Lord didn't need to fast, but He fasted on behalf of all humanity. The Lord wants us to follow His steps and learn how to conquer the devil.

The Lord Jesus addresses fasting on His Sermon on the Mount. When John the Baptist's disciples asked the Lord Christ, "Why do we and the Pharisees fast often, but Your disciples do not fast?" Jesus said to them, "Can the friends of the bridegroom mourn as long as the bridegroom is with them? But the days will come when the bridegroom will be taken away from them, and then they will fast."(Matt. 9: 14 – 15)

Again, the Lord mentioned fasting by saying, "This kind can come out by nothing but prayer and fasting."

(Mark 9: 29) This is the secret of victory in our spiritual struggle.

The Book of Acts talks about the fasting of the church of Antioch (Acts 13: 3) and how St Paul fasted as he was heading towards Italy. (Acts 27) St. Paul mentions fasting in many parts of his Epistles, "But in all things we commend ourselves as ministers of God: in much patience, in tribulations, in needs, in distresses, in stripes, in imprisonments, in tumults, in labors, in sleeplessness, in fastings; by purity, by knowledge, by longsuffering, by kindness, by the Holy Spirit, by sincere love..." (Cor. 6: 4,5) Again he mentions "fasting" to the Corinthians, "... in weariness and toil, in sleeplessness often, in hunger and thirst, in fastings often, in cold and nakedness..." (2 Cor. 11: 27) He also addresses husbands and wives saying, "Do not deprive one another except with consent for a time, that you may give yourselves to fasting and prayer; and come together again so that Satan does not tempt you because of your lack of self-control." (1 Cor. 7: 5)

IN THE LIVES OF THE CHURCH FATHERS

The importance of fasting is clear in the lives and sayings of the church fathers. History is full of biographies of strong men and women of God who reached a high spiritual level by practicing fasting.

All the saints practiced fasting and penned down their experiences. Many of these saints were called 'The Fasters', being renowned for their remarkable fasting.

• It was said about St Basil the Great, Archbishop of Caesarea, that he never ate meat during his religious reign. He used to wear sackcloth under his clothes while saying: "We were expelled from earthly Paradise because we did not fast, so we have to fast in order to go back to the heavenly Paradise. Fasting reconciles us with God." He also says: "Fasting controlled the fire for the Three young youth and shut the mouths of lions for Daniel."

• St John Chrysostom, the Pope of Constantinople, always ate soaked beans during his Papacy. He says: "Fasting is victorious because it fights on our behalf against our enemies. It takes us to our real freedom."

Let's meditate on the lives of hermits and ascetics. They fled the world and resorted to the mountains where they lived in caves. They befriended fasting all the days of their lives, and in turn, fasting turned them into angels.

• Moses and Elijah practiced fasting. Thus, they were honoured in seeing the Lord in His Transfiguration.

• St Ambrose, Bishop of Milan, talks about the 40 days of Holy Lent, saying, "Jesus Christ, Who was sinless, fasted 40 days. What about you, the sinner? Fasting for forty days provides a flood of divine blessings. The power of fasting drowns our sins and preserves holiness in our hearts."

• St Jerome says: "The Lord Himself sanctified His Baptism by fasting 40 days. He taught us to conquer the devil by fasting and prayer." In a letter to the virgin, Dimitrias, he wrote: "We have so many Divine witnesses in the Holy Bible concerning gluttony and love of food and clothing. The first human ignored God's instructions and followed his gluttony for food, thus he was expelled from Paradise to the land of tears and troubles. Since gluttony blocked our way to Paradise, let us try to return to our original state through asceticism."

• Saint Isaac says: "Fasting is the first step towards a holy life with God. It is the straightening of all virtues, the beginning of struggle, the beauty of celibacy, the protection of chastity, the father of prayer, the source of serenity, the teacher of silence and the announcer of good things." He also says: "God has burnished this weapon of fasting, so who would dare despise it?! If the Giver of the Law Himself fasted, how could we ignore fasting??!"

• St. Gregory the Archimandrite of Cyprus says: "Evil dreams sadden the heart of he who eats a lot, but he who eats little by little is alert at all times. The brain in dimmed because of too much food, just like clouds which make a thick fog in the sky."

THE MIGHT OF FASTING

One of the most fascinating fasts was the fasting of the city of Nineveh. Although God had already decided to destroy the city, when He saw their deep humiliation, He didn't carry out its destruction but had mercy on them, "Then God saw their works, that they turned from their evil way; and God relented from the disaster that He had said He would bring upon them, and He did not do it." (Jonah 3: 10)

Could God ever regret? The preservation of the city of Nineveh from destruction shows the effectiveness of fasting. Everyone in Nineveh fasted, including the children and infants, together with the king who wore sackcloth and sat on the dust. The animals fasted and wore sackcloth as well. Everyone cried fervently to the Lord and so He had mercy upon them.

St. John Chrysostom comments on this incident saying: "God honours fasting and delivers those who also honour fasting. Fasting has a special authority and power. Although the Lord was ready to destroy Nineveh, He changed his decision, based on the fasting of the people."

God talked to Isaiah the Prophet about the core of fasting and its suitable practice. He also talked about its blessings, might and promises, "Then your light shall break forth like the morning, your healing shall spring forth speedily, and your righteousness shall go before you; the glory of the LORD shall be your rear guard. Then you shall call, and the Lord will answer; you shall cry, and He will say, 'Here I am.'" (Isaiah 58: 8, 9) How wonderful are the promises of fasting...

WHY DO WE FAST?

TOO MUCH FOOD AROUSES THE DESIRES

There is a strong relationship between the energy of people and how they act. Strong people can quickly get aggravated because they have more energy than necessary. The energy of people is related to what they eat. St. John Cassian says: "The seeds of debauch grow when the stomach is full of food. The mind suffocates out of fullness and cannot direct or control the thoughts. Gluttony does not only drunk the mind, but withdraws the mind from pure meditation. The reason behind the destruction and abomination of the city of Sodom was gluttony. This is clear from the Lord's words: "Look, this was the iniquity of your sister Sodom: She and her daughter had pride, fullness of food." (Ez. 16:49) Therefore, those who satisfied their bodily desires were burnt with sulphur and fire.

FASTING IS A BRIDE TO THE BODY

Our body is full of different materialistic desires. It pulls a person down and forces him to sin; "For the flesh lusts against the Spirit, and the Spirit against the flesh; and these are contrary to one another, so that you do not do the things that you wish." (Gal. 5: 17) Also, "For the good that I will to do, I do not do; but the evil I will not to do, that I practice. Now if I do what I will not to do, it is no longer I who do it, but sin that dwells in me.

"I find then a law, that evil is present with me, the

one who wills to do good. For I delight in the law of God according to the inward man. But I see another law in my members, warring against the law of my mind, and bringing me into captivity to the law of sin which is in my members. O wretched man that I am! Who will deliver me from this body of death?" (Rom. 7: 19 – 24)

We need strong control of the body through different means, and the best of these is fasting. Our saintly fathers experienced this fact. St Isaac says: "Any struggle against sin and its desires should start with fasting, especially if we are struggling against an inner sin." St Ironimus says: "God's aim from fasting is not to make us suffer hunger, but to pave the way to chastity!!" Saint John of Assiut says: "Fasting conquers desires just as water quenches fire." A saintly father says: "The enemy attacks the heart through the fullness of the stomach."

FASTING IS THE BEGINNING OF THE SPIRITUAL LIFE

Man is formed from spirit and body. Depending on which one overcomes the other, a person becomes either a spiritual or bodily one. If a person wants to be spiritual, he should subdue and submit his body. Our Saviour Jesus Christ gave us an example when He fasted after His Baptism in the Jordan River. Thus, all those who "walk in newness of life," (Rom. 6: 4) start their spiritual life with fasting.

"Then Jesus was led up by the Spirit into the wilderness" where He fasted. (Matt. 4: 1) St Isaac says: "When our Lord revealed Himself to the world after His Baptism, He headed to the wilderness and fasted for forty days and forty nights. All those who want to follow His steps should build their struggle according to His example."

St. John Cassian penned a wonderful experience saying: "We can never start a battle with our inner man unless we get rid of the vice of gluttony. We have to prove that we are released from the dominion of the body, "While they promise them liberty, they themselves are slaves of corruption; for by whom a person is overcome, by him also he is brought into bondage." (2 Peter 2: 17) Furthermore, "Jesus answered them, "Most assuredly, I say to you, whoever commits sin is a slave of sin." (John 8: 34)

A full stomach can never fight the inner man. St Paul the Apostle always concentrated on subduing the body. He says: "Therefore I run thus: not with uncertainty. Thus I fight: not as one who beats the air. But I discipline my body and bring it into subjection, lest, when I have preached to others, I myself should become disqualified." (1 Cor. 9: 26, 27) Our great enemy is within ourselves. We risk our lives daily in an inner fight. If we win our inner war, we can overcome any outer war. Conquer your inner wars by the authority of the Spirit.

FASTING PAVES THE WAY TO VIRTUE AND TALENT

If fasting is the beginning of the spiritual life, it is therefore the pavement for virtues. It opens the door for virtue and it ornaments the soul. St Filoxinus says: "The more ascetic the body is, the stronger the Spirit. Little food makes the body light and subdues it to the authority of the soul."

In the past, holy books were written on scripts made of animal skin. These skins had to be cleaned, flattened and made appropriate for writing, otherwise they would not be used. It is the same with the human soul. The soul needs to be cleaned and prepared through fasting and asceticism, otherwise God will not engrave His words into it.

Isaiah the Prophet says, "Whom will he teach knowledge? And whom will he make to understand the message? Those just weaned from milk? Those just drawn from the breasts?" (Is. 28: 9) Who are those weaned from milk and who are those drawn from the breast except those who give up the luxuries of the world and subdue themselves to fasting and uprightness.

Any weak wind can lift up a feather if it is not attached to something. However if the feather is wet or attached to any animal, the wind can never blow it away. In the same way, a person who is indulged with lust and tied up to bodily desires, can never lift his soul and mind to heaven. Our Lord Jesus Christ warns us saying, "But take heed to yourselves, lest your hearts be weighed down with carousing, drunkenness, and cares of this life, and that Day come on you unexpectedly." (Luke 21:34)

The same thing is noticed if we throw a green branch in fire. The wet branch doesn't catch fire straight away. It takes time for the fire to remove the humility and then burn the branch. However, a dry branch will catch fire immediately. Similarly, a person might be regular in practising spiritual means, yet he is lukewarm and lacking in God's comforts. The fire of Divine Love cannot inflame one's heart unless he rids himself of all bodily desires, through fasting and other ascetic practices.

FASTING TAMES THE BODY AND THE SENSES

David the Prophet says: "But as for me, when they were sick, my clothing was sackcloth; I humbled myself with fasting; and my prayer would return to my own heart." (Ps. 35: 13) St Paul uses another expression to prove the effectiveness of fasting, "But I discipline my body and bring it into subjection, lest, when I have preached to others, I myself should become disqualified." (1 Cor.9: 27)

To control a revolution, the government arrests the rebellions and imprisons them. This is exactly what fasting does to our body. It calms the body and controls rebellious senses. In addition, fasting leads to the purity of the soul. St. John Cassian says: "Our early fathers practised fasting daily to purify their souls and hearts. They forbad us from gluttony and fullness of stomach, even with just plain bread and water."

FASTING STRENGTHENS THE WILL

We fall into sin due to our weak will. Fasting strengthens our "will" and teaches self-control. Abstaining from food for a certain period of time is the most effective way by which the human will is strengthened. When a person abstains from food, he does not respond to the desire of his body, thus he is able to block out any other desire.

How to Fast?

Control the desires

Fasting is a means to subdue the body, resist evil and control lustful desires. In Coptic, the word "fasting" means "to tie the inside." In this context, the "inside" refers to the desires.

St. John Cassian says: "We have to care a lot about fasting because it paves the way to purity of heart."

St Filoxinous says: "If your eye desires anything placed on the table, do not touch it. If you train your body this way, it will only ask for its essential needs. It is better to eat meat without desire than to eat lentils with enjoyment."

St. John Cassian penned wonderful words about fasting . He says, "Fasting from certain kinds of food does not produce purity of heart unless it is accompanied with the fasting of the soul. Gossip is one of the soul's favourite meals, and so is anger, jealousy, envy and hatred. These are all miserable kinds of food which lead to destruction. If we abstain from these harmful things, our bodily fasting will be useful and fruitful. The weariness of the body, together with the humbleness of the soul, are an acceptable sacrifice to the Lord. It produces a store of holiness and purity in the depths of the inner heart."

However, if we fast from certain foods, while still being tied to certain sins, we will not gain any benefit from fasting. We need to fast both body and heart. "For this reason I bow my knees to the Father of our Lord Jesus

Christ, from whom the whole family in heaven and earth is named, that He would grant you, according to the riches of His glory, to be strengthened with might through His Spirit in the inner man, that Christ may dwell in your hearts through faith; that you, being rooted and grounded in love..." (Eph. 3: 14 – 17)

How easy is it too fast from certain kinds of food, but how hard is it to fast from a certain sin or lust. Blessed is the person who fasts from the sins of the soul. Without a doubt, he will be nourished with spiritual food and will say: "My food is to do God's will!!"

HUMILIATION

The aim of fasting is to control and discipline one's self. This cannot be done without repentance, regret and humiliation. David the Prophet and Kings says: "But as for me, when they were sick, my clothing was sackcloth; I humbled myself with fasting; and my prayer would return to my own heart." (Ps. 35: 13) St Ironimus says: "After David committed adultery and his son fell sick, he sat among the ashes and fasted saying, "For I have eaten ashes like bread, and mingled my drink with weeping." (Ps 102: 9) Also, "My knees are weak through fasting, and my flesh is feeble from lack of fatness." (Ps 109:24) Isaiah the Prophet addresses the importance of humility in Fasting.

"Why have we fasted," they say, "and You have not seen?

Why have we afflicted our souls, and You take no notice?"

"In fact, in the day of your fast, you find pleasure,

And exploit all your labourers.

Indeed you fast for strife and debate,

And to strike with the fist of wickedness.

You will not fast as you do this day,

To make your voice heard on high.

Is it a fast that I have chosen,

A day for a man to afflict his soul?

Is it to bow down his head like a bulrush,

And to spread out sackcloth and ashes?

Would you call this a fast,

And an acceptable day to the LORD?

"Is this not the fast that I have chosen:

To loose the bonds of wickedness,

To undo the heavy burdens,

To let the oppressed go free,

And that you break every yoke?" (Is. 58: 3-5)

That's how the children of God comprehend fasting, and know how to win God's mercy. The citizens of Nineveh obtained God's mercy when their hearts were moved with repentance after Jonah's call, "So the people of Nineveh believed God, proclaimed a fast, and put on sackcloth, from the greatest to the least of them. Then word came to the king of Nineveh; and he arose from his throne and laid aside his robe, covered himself with sackcloth and sat in ashes. And he caused it to be proclaimed and published throughout Nineveh by the decree of the king and his nobles, saying, Let neither man nor beast, herd nor flock, taste anything; do not let them eat, or drink water. But let man and beast be covered with sackcloth, and cry mightily to God; yes, let everyone turn from his evil way and from the violence that is in his hands." (Jonah 3: 5-8)

Humility coming out of a repentant soul pleases the Lord. When Elijah informed the king about the disasters and calamities coming upon him and his household, Jezebel, King Ahab's wife, said: "You now exercise authority over Israel! Arise, eat food, and let your heart be cheerful; I will give you the vineyard of Naboth the Jezreelite." And she wrote letters in Ahab's name, sealed them with his seal, and sent the letters to the elders and the nobles who were dwelling in the city with Naboth. She wrote in the letters, saying, Proclaim a fast, and seat Naboth with high honour among the people. (1 Kings 21: 7-9)

For this reason, Fasting is practiced during times of hardships and during times organised by the church and guided by the Holy Spirit. (See 2 Sam. 1: 12, Daniel 6: 18, 2 Sam. 12: 16, Esther 4: 16)

FASTING AND THE PERIODS OF ABSTAINING

Fasting should be practiced with abstaining. There is no real fasting if there is no period of abstinence. The core of fasting lies in the period of abstaining; its meaning, aim, practices and results. A Christian who has a vegetarian breakfast might think that he is fasting, but actually he is not. Moreover, he is breaching an important aspect of fasting, which is 'abstaining.'

Fasting involves feeling hungry, not just refraining from certain kinds of food. When our Lord fasted, it is written, "....and when He had fasted forty days and forty nights, afterward He was hungry." (Matt. 4: 2) In the book of Acts, it is written about Peter the Apostle:"Then he became very hungry and wanted to eat, but while they made ready, he fell into a trance."(Acts 10: 10) Even in the Old Testament, Moses fasted with abstinence; "So he was there with the Lord forty days and forty nights; he neither ate bread nor drank water. And He wrote on the tablets the words of the covenant, the Ten Commandments." (Ex. 34:28)

In the book of Judges, fasting lasted until night, "Then all the children of Israel, that is, all the people, went up and came to the house of God and wept. They sat there before the Lord and fasted that day until evening; and they offered burnt offerings and peace offerings before the Lord." (Judges 20: 26) When the Lord explained to Ezekiel the Prophet how to fast, He said, "And your food which you eat shall be by weight, twenty shekels a day; from time to time you shall eat it. You shall also drink water by measure, one-sixth of a hin; from time to time you shall drink."(Ez. 4: 10, 11) When the people of Nineveh fasted, they ate nothing!! (Jonah 3: 7)

MODERATION IN FASTING

In Christianity, fasting is not mandatory, but we do it because we feel the need to do so. We are not supposed to fix times for abstaining except under the guidance of the confession father. Fasting can lead to dangerous results if it is not done properly. The early fathers say: "Do not extremely weaken your body lest your enemies mock you."

All saints recommended fasting in moderation. In a letter to Dimetrias the virgin, St. Ironimus wrote: "No matter the situation, I am not going to fast in excess because this will weaken the body quickly and cause disease. Reduce your abstinence if you start feeling fast heart beats and drowsiness. You have to keep enough energy for the reading of the Holy Bible, the singing of Psalms and the alertness of the mind. Fasting is not a virtue, but it is a base on which other virtues are built. It is a step to a higher road."

St Isaac says: "Beware lest you weaken your body through excess fasting. This will make you lazy and lukewarm. Weigh your life on the scale of knowledge." Fasting under harsh conditions and without discernment or guidance will weaken and destroy the body. It can cause the mind to lose control.

St. John Cassian says: "We are all different in bodily needs, energy and age, so there is no general rule for fasting and abstinence. However, all types of fasting produce body control."

Special cases are nursing mothers, the pregnant and the elderly due to their weak and fragile bodies. St John Cassian says: "Weakness of the body doesn't stop the purity of the heart. So long as the individual is not eating food with enjoyment."

The priests of the Church are given authority by God

to permit someone to break his/her fast or to organise it in a certain way, based on bodily need and spiritual level.

FASTING AND DIFFERENT KINDS OF FOOD

In addition to the abstaining periods, a person must refrain from eating certain types of food. The church has received this tradition from the Apostles.

When Elijah escaped from Jezebel; "Then as he lay and slept under a broom tree, suddenly an angel touched him, and said to him, "Arise and eat." Then he looked, and there by his head was a cake baked on coals, and a jar of water. So he ate and drank, and lay down again. And the angel of the Lord came back the second time, and touched him, and said, "Arise and eat, because the journey is too great for you." So he arose, and ate and drank; and he went in the strength of that food forty days and forty nights as far as Horeb, the mountain of God." (1 Kings 19: 5-8) Wasn't God capable of sending some wine, cooked food or meat?

Similarly, Daniel the Prophet could have eaten from the delicious food offered at the king's table, "but Daniel purposed in his heart that he would not defile himself with the portion of the king's delicacies, nor with the wine which he drank; therefore he requested of the chief of the eunuchs that he might not defile himself." (Dan 1:8)

Giving up certain foods in fasting is a vital matter; it helps in chastising the soul and limiting its cravings. We cannot abstain and then eat whatever we like for this will make us more greedy and will increase our gluttony. Seafood is allowed in certain fasting periods. This is because fish reproduce without desire. The fertilization process takes place outside the body of the female.

Fasting does not weaken the body

Some people presume that vegetarian food weakens the body because of its low nutrition substances. However, this is not the case. You feel hungry during fasting times because your mind is concentrating on your body and as soon as your stomach empties, you notice feelings of hunger. The person who is occupied with heavenly matters does not concentrate on his hunger. His soul is filled and so it lifts up the body.

Sometimes we forget to eat if we are busy with a specific issue. David the Prophet says: "Thus I will bless You while I live; I will lift up my hands in Your name. My soul shall be satisfied as with marrow and fatness, and my mouth shall praise You with joyful lips."

It is not only joy in the Lord which fills the soul, but also sadness for our sins, "My heart is stricken and withered like grass, so that I forget to eat my bread." (Ps. 102: 4) King Solomon says: "A satisfied soul loathes the honeycomb, but to a hungry soul every bitter thing is sweet." (Prov. 27: 7) Notice that he says the soul and not body.

The body gets filled if the soul is already filled. Therefore, a natural fasting will proceed, without obligation or hunger. Isn't it amazing that the materialistic body gets filled by non materialistic things?! I feel sorry for the person who fasts with his body, yet does not offer divine nutrition for his soul. Joel the prophet says: "Blow the trumpet in Zion, consecrate a fast, call a sacred assembly."(Joel 2: 15) Retreats are supposedly good opportunities for prayer and fasting, both of which lead us on the path to eternity.

How could our saintly fathers abstain from food for days and at the same time, perform numerous prostrations?? Actually, they were supported by heavenly grace. The grace of God gave them continuous support. As their body performs spiritual practises, it gets nourished by the food of the Spirit. This was experienced by Daniel and the three youth. Although they insisted on eating vegetarian meals, they were nourished by the food of their Spirit, "But Daniel purposed in his heart that he would not defile himself with the portion of the king's delicacies, nor with the wine which he drank; therefore he requested of the chief of the eunuchs that he might not defile himself. Now God had brought Daniel into the favor and goodwill of the chief of the eunuchs. And the chief of the eunuchs said to Daniel, "I fear my lord the king, who has appointed your food and drink. For why should he see your faces looking worse than the young men who are your age? Then you would endanger my head before the king." So Daniel said to the steward whom the chief of the eunuchs had set over Daniel, Hananiah, Mishael, and Azariah, "Please test your servants for ten days, and let them give us vegetables to eat and water to drink. Then let our appearance be examined before you, and the appearance of the young men who eat the portion of the king's delicacies; and as you see fit, so deal with your servants." So he consented with them in this matter, and tested them ten days. And at the end of ten days their features appeared better and fatter in flesh than all the young men who ate the portion of the king's delicacies. Thus the steward took away their portion of delicacies and the wine that they were to drink, and gave them vegetables." (Dan.1: 8–15) Therefore, strong belief in

God's promises, together with a spiritual attitude, supports the body during struggle.

Fasting and Spiritual Practices

The saints based their lives on spiritual practices, "But when they had commanded them to go aside out of the council, they conferred among themselves, saying, "What shall we do to these men? For, indeed, that a notable miracle has been done through them is evident to all who dwell in Jerusalem, and we cannot deny it."(Acts 4: 16) Fasting is considered the best pavement for other spiritual practices. The aim is to get the soul used to certain good virtues. However if the body is a troublesome one, it is very hard to achieve any good result. Thus fasting, subdues and humiliates the body, allowing for the practice of new virtues.

Companionship of Fasting and Prayer

The Lord Jesus Christ says: "This kind can come out by nothing but prayer and fasting,"(Mark 9: 29) which highlights the importance of fasting and prayer being performed together. "Then, having fasted and prayed, and laid hands on them, they sent them away.(Acts 13: ,3) Moreover, "So when they had appointed elders in every church, and prayed with fasting, they commended them to the Lord in whom they had believed."(Acts 14: 23) St Paul addresses married couples by saying: "Do not deprive one another except with consent for a time, that you may give yourselves to fasting and prayer; and come together again so that Satan does not tempt you because of your lack of self-control.(1 Cor. 7: 5)

The early fathers resembled fasting to a fortress and prayer to a weapon. St Augustine says: "King Solomon made two altars in the Temple: one outside for offering sacrifices, and the other one inside for incense offerings. Similarly, human beings are temples of the Holy Spirit. They should have two altars; an inner altar (the heart) on which the incense of prayers is offered, and an outer altar which is the body, for the offering of fasting and asceticism."

With the same meaning St. Paul says, "I beseech you therefore, brethren, by the mercies of God, that you present your bodies a living sacrifice, holy, acceptable to God, which is your reasonable service."(Rom. 12: 1)

Solomon the King writes, "Who is this coming out of the wilderness like pillars of smoke, perfumed with myrrh and frankincense, with all the merchant's fragrant powders?"(Song of Songs 3: 6)

In this case, he is referring to the victorious human soul. It is perfumed with myrrh as a sign of fasting, and frankincense as a sign of prayer. Some people question if myrrh (fasting) is a perfume? Yes it is!! Fasting and asceticism is a sweet aroma which cleanses the soul from the rot of sin and gives it the sweet smell of Christ. If we resemble fasting with fire coal, then prayer is the incense. They both complete each other. A nice smell comes out of their combination, perfuming the human soul.

FASTING AND ALMSGIVING

The Lord Jesus organised the three corners of Christianity in His Sermon on the Mount: Prayer, Fasting and Almsgiving. Fasting is attached to prayer and almsgiving. All three are necessary before God. The Lord mentioned this to Isaiah the Prophet: "Is this not the fast that I have chosen: to loose the bonds of wickedness, to undo the heavy burdens, to let the oppressed go free, and that you break every yoke? Is it not to share your bread with the hungry, and that you bring to your house the poor who are cast out; when you see the naked, that you cover him, and not hide yourself from your own flesh?" (Is. 58: 6, 7)

He also said to Ezekiel the Prophet, "Look, this was the iniquity of your sister Sodom: She and her daughter had pride, fullness of food, and abundance of idleness; neither did she strengthen the hand of the poor and needy."(Ez. 16: 49)

FASTING AND MARITAL RELATIONSHIPS

Since fasting involves subduing the body, the church considers it a broken fast if there is a relationship held during the fasting period. This does not mean that a marital relationship is something defiled, but it does break the fast. People give it up as a kind of asceticism, exactly like giving up food. It is written, "Blow the trumpet in Zion, consecrate a fast, call a sacred assembly. Gather the people, sanctify the congregation, assemble the elders, gather the children and nursing babes; Let the bridegroom go out from his chamber, and the bride from her dressing room." (Joel 2: 15, 16)

ADVICES AND GUIDELINES

1. You have to practice fasting according to your confession father's guidance, especially for periods of abstaining.

2. The aim of fasting is not to weaken the body, because we have to look after our bodies. It is well known that a sound mind is in a healthy body. God calls us to subdue the body, not to kill it, and so, the church does not allow abstinence for the elderly, toddlers, nursing mothers, pregnant women and young children. They are not expected to fast abstinence because eating is a physical necessity for them.

The body is the mule which takes you through the wilderness of this world. Do not let it be a haggard animal lest it should rebel and throw you away. On the other hand, do not be extra harsh lest it should not finish the way with you, but, "Let all things be done decently and in order." (1 Cor. 14: 40)

3. Do not try to apply everything you have read here, because we all have different spiritual and physical levels. Remember the Apostle's words: "For I say, through the grace given to me, to everyone who is among you, not to think of himself more highly than he ought to think, but to think soberly, as God has dealt to each one a measure of faith." (Romans 12: 3)

Spiritual life needs a lot of practice and gradual ascent. It is excellent to yearn to imitate the saints, but also look at their beginnings, and how they gradually reached a high spiritual level.

4. Sick and weak people are special cases. St Parsonofius says: "You should know that fasting humiliates the body, but if the body is already humiliated with illness, we have already reached the aim of fasting."

5. Beware of pretending you are sick to skip fasting. Do not deceive yourself into sickness when your body is strong, and do not refrain from fasting for fear your body will get weak. On the contrary, fasting makes you healthier and more active; most vegetarian people live longer.

St Ironimus says: "It is better to have a sick stomach than a sick soul. It is better to have shaky knees than shaky chastity, so subdue your body and humiliate it lest you should be dismissed."

St John Cassian says: "It is strange how we care alot about our body and health, yet we still fall sick. However, the saints humiliated their bodies with fasting, yet they led a healthier life. It is strange how our bodies rot after death, while saint bodies stay concrete and spread a sweet aroma."

6. Do not crave certain foods while fasting. Lots of people eat delicious food that can't be differentiate from non fasting foods. We should have some asceticism and piety in fasting. Deal with your body as a doctor would deal with a sick patient. Do not allow harmful things to enter your body even if your body yearns for it.

7. Remember to fast from a certain sin or bad habit such as anger, judgement or lust.

8. Accompany fasting with meditation. For example,

think about how Judas betrayed Christ. Then, think about yourself. Do you betray Christ with your sins? Do you add to the thorns of His head? Do you nail His hands more? Do you scourge His back again and again?

9. If you want your fasting to be acceptable, you should offer it clear from any iniquity or hypocrisy. The Scribes and Pharisees used to fast, yet the Lord rejected their fasting because it was full of hypocrisy. "Also He spoke this parable to some who trusted in themselves that they were righteous, and despised others: "Two men went up to the temple to pray, one a Pharisee and the other a tax collector. The Pharisee stood and prayed thus with himself, 'God, I thank You that I am not like other men—extortioners, unjust, adulterers, or even as this tax collector. I fast twice a week; I give tithes of all that I possess.' And the tax collector, standing afar off, would not so much as raise his eyes to heaven, but beat his breast, saying, 'God, be merciful to me a sinner!' I tell you, this man went down to his house justified rather than the other; for everyone who exalts himself will be humbled, and he who humbles himself will be exalted."(Luke 18: 9-14)

The Lord does not accept the fasting of evil people either. "Thus says the Lord to this people: "Thus they have loved to wander; They have not restrained their feet. Therefore the Lord does not accept them; He will remember their iniquity now, And punish their sins." Then the LORD said to me, "Do not pray for this people, for their good. When they fast, I will not hear their cry; and when they offer burnt offering and grain offering, I will not accept them. But I will consume them by the sword, by the famine, and by the pestilence." (Jer.14: 10-12)

FASTING IN THE ORTHODOX CHURCH

1. The most important fasts are the Holy Lent, Passion Week and Wednesdays and Fridays. This is mentioned in the Disqolia [Teachings of the Apostles] and the teachings of St Basil the Great and others. The church was always strict in carrying these fasts. The Holy Lent was fasted by the Lord Himself, Wednesday is for the commemoration of the conspiracy, Friday for His Crucifixion and Passion Week for His sufferings and pains.

2. The Apostles' Fasting was a fast done by the Apostles themselves and it was a bit different than the fast known today. It is written in the Disqolia that they celebrated the Descent of the Holy Spirit for a week, then fasted for a week or two. However today, the Apostles' Fasting does not have a fixed number of days as it is connected with the Holy 50 Days which differ from year to year.

3. The rest of the Church's Fasts are:

• The Advent: is a fast for 43 days starting from 16th Hatour (25th November) and ending on Christmas Day, 29th Kiahk (7th January).

• Nineveh Fasting (Jonah): is a three day fast, in commemoration of the repentance of the people of Nineveh. It occurs two weeks before the Holy Lent.

• St Mary's Fasting: is a fast for 15 days ending on the Feast of the Assumption of St Mary's body on 16th Misra.

• Nativity and Epiphany Paramoun: The day

preceding the Feast of Nativity or the Feast of Epiphany. People abstain from food throughout the day in order to gain blessings on these two great feasts.

4. These fasts differ in their rites, periods of abstinence and the type of food that can be eaten. Seafood is forbidden in the Holy Lent, Wednesdays and Fridays, Nineveh fasting and the Paramoun. During Passion Week, the church rite encourages bread and salt after abstinence. As for the sick and weak, they are not permitted to abstain. However, they are forbidden from sweets and desserts. Seafood is allowed in all other fasts.

5. During Holy Lent, the period of abstinence should be till sunset at 6pm. All other fasts have an abstinence period until 3pm. However, abstinence periods should be in consultation with the confession father.

6. Abstaining from food is forbidden during Saturdays and Sundays throughout the entire year, except on Joyous Saturday where Lord Jesus was lying in the tomb. Fasting is forbidden during the 50 Holy Days following Easter. This is the only period where we break the fast of Wednesdays and Fridays.

7. Prostrations befit fasting. So when fasting is forbidden on certain days, prostrations are also forbidden, such as the Major Lordly Feasts, 50 Holy Days, and Saturdays and Sundays.

Almsgiving

x

> "Blessed is he who considers the poor, the Lord
> will deliver him in time of trouble."
> (Ps. 41: 1)

- ❧ Introduction on Almsgiving
- ❧ God orders Almsgiving
- ❧ How to offer Almsgiving
- ❧ Tithes
- ❧ Objections concerning Tithes
- ❧ Examples of Generous Almsgiving personalities

INTRODUCTION TO ALMSGIVING

Christianity and almsgiving can never be separated from each other. Materialistic almsgiving has little value compared to offering oneself. This is the sublime nature of Almsgiving.

Almsgiving, together with prayer and fasting, forms a strong braid of three strings. If we are connected to almsgiving, we are sure of true salvation. Through prayers, we worship God with our spirits. Through fasting, we worship Him with our bodies. Through almsgiving, we express our love to Him through Giving.

Almsgiving was an early Church principle since the beginning of Christianity. It is clear in St Paul's words to the priests of Ephesus, "I have shown you in every way, by labouring like this, that you must support the weak. And remember the words of the Lord Jesus, that He said, 'It is more blessed to give than to receive.'" (Acts 20: 35)

Here, we will concentrate on charity. That is, Almsgiving. In this materialistic world, people are obsessed over material things. We notice that people are becoming less enthusiastic about giving, in stark contrast to early Christianity when the believers used to sell all their possessions and offer it to the church. We know that poor and needy people are suffering. We also know about the numerous blessings prepared by the Lord to those who are merciful; in this world and hereafter. Then, why don't we give?

GOD AND MONEY

Money is a great god during this day and age as it is adored by many. It misleads and hardens the hearts of many, blinding their hearts and deafening their ears from the cries of those who are suffering. This god has become so strong, because people now worship it over the true God. Our Great God, Who knows the hearts of human beings says, "You cannot serve God and mammon." (Luke 16: 13)

When the rich man approached the Lord Jesus, and asked about the way which leads to eternal life, Jesus answered, "One thing you lack: Go your way, sell whatever you have and give to the poor, and you will have treasure in heaven." St Mark then says: "But he was sad at this word, and went away sorrowful, for he had great possessions." Christ commented on this incident by saying, "Children, how hard it is for those who trust in riches to enter the kingdom of God! It is easier for a camel to go through the eye of a needle than for a rich man to enter the kingdom of God."(Mark 10: 17-25)

Lord Jesus also says, "Take heed and beware of covetousness, for one's life does not consist in the abundance of the things he possesses."(Luke 12: 15) He also says, "So likewise, whoever of you does not forsake all that he has, cannot be My disciple." (Luke 14: 33) Therefore, the love and dependence on money, is a very dangerous spiritual disease which separates us from our God and His fellowship.

Someone might say that the Lord didn't literally mean the "rich people" when He says, 'those who trust in riches.' This is true, because the Lord is the source of all riches,"the

Lord makes poor and makes rich." (1 Sam. 2: 7) Also, "As for every man to whom God has given riches and wealth, and given him power to eat of it, to receive his heritage and rejoice in his labour—this is the gift of God." (Ecc. 5: 19)

The Holy Bible mentions names of some saints who were rich. For example, Abraham, about whom it was said, "Abraham was very rich in livestock, in silver and in gold." (Gen. 13: 2) Lot was also rich (Gen. 13: 5, 6) and same with Isaac, as the Lord blessed his plantations; "Then Isaac sowed in that land, and reaped in the same year a hundredfold; and the Lord blessed him." Furthermore, "The man began to prosper, and continued prospering until he became very prosperous." (Gen. 26)

The Lord blessed Joseph and he became the lord of Pharaoh's house and a ruler throughout all the land of Egypt. (Genesis 45) It is also written about David, "So he died in a good old age, full of days and riches and honour." (1 Chr. 29: 28) Moreover, Jehoshaphat had riches and honour in abundance. (2 Chr. 17: 5) Hezekiah "had very great riches and honour. And he made himself treasuries for silver, for gold, for precious stones, for spices, for shields, and for all kinds of desirable items."(2 Chr. 32: 27) Job was also wealthy as "his possessions were seven thousand sheep, three thousand camels, five hundred yoke of oxen, five hundred female donkeys, and a very large household, so that this man was the greatest of all the people of the East." (Job 1: 3) Similarly, Joseph of Arimathea was rich in that he took Jesus' body and wrapped it in clean linen cloth. Zaccheus became rich when Jesus visited his house. (Luke 19: 2) Going back to the words of Jesus, "Those who trust in riches..."

TRUSTING IN RICHES

It is the feeling of being safe and comfortable for having so much money. It is thinking that by your power and riches, you can overcome calamities and unexpected circumstances. A rich person knows that the poor are in need of his/her excessive riches, but the feeling of safety and comfort is the reason why he/she keeps the riches, rather than gives it out. Therefore, anyone who depends on their money and collects it for preservation, is fulfilling the Lord's words, "Children, how hard it is for those who trust in riches to enter the kingdom of God."

The desire of becoming rich is one of the most dangerous temptations as it can totally destroy, "But those who desire to be rich, fall into temptation and a snare, and into many foolish and harmful lusts which drown men in destruction and perdition. For the love of money is a root of all kinds of evil, for which some have strayed from the faith in their greediness, and pierced themselves through with many sorrows. But you, O man of God, flee these things and pursue righteousness, godliness, faith, love, patience, gentleness." (1 Tim. 6: 11)

The Lord also commanded His children in the Old Testament saying, "Beware that you do not forget the LORD your God by not keeping His commandments, His judgments, and His statutes which I command you today, lest—when you have eaten and are full, and have built beautiful houses and dwell in them; and when your herds and your flocks multiply, and your silver and your gold are multiplied, and all that you have is multiplied; when your heart is lifted up, and you forget the LORD your God who brought you out of the land of Egypt, from the house of bondage." (Deut. 8: 11-14)

The Lord of Glory says, "For where your treasure is, there your heart will be also."(Luke 12: 34) Moreover, "No one can serve two masters; for either he will hate the one and love the other, or else he will be loyal to the one and despise the other. You cannot serve God and mammon." (Matt.6: 24) Will you still reject these verses and say that you are capable of serving God and mammon?

Even if a rich man does not "love" his money but keeps it for himself without satisfying the needs of the poor, he is still contradicting Christianity and its main principle of love. A Christian believer is the one who has died to the love of the world, because it is written, "For we brought nothing into this world, and it is certain we can carry nothing out." (1 Tim.6: 7) The Apostle wrote these words for all believers, not only to a certain denomination, especially because there were no monks during this era.

A christian should love his neighbour as himself. The rich who refuse to help the needy, show a lack of love for their neighbour, "But whoever has this world's goods, and sees his brother in need, and shuts up his heart from him, how does the love of God abide in him?(John 1: 3: 17) Moreover, "Come now, you rich, weep and howl for your miseries that are coming upon you! Your riches are corrupted, and your garments are moth-eaten."(James 5: 1)

St. Jerome wrote a letter to Youstikom, a noble virgin in Rome, saying: "You have to avoid loving money. If you are not honest in what is not yours, then how can you be honest in what IS yours?" The things that are not yours include worldly silver and gold, but what is yours is an eternal inheritance about which is written," Poverty and shame will come to him who disdains correction, but he who regards a rebuke will be honoured." (Prov. 13: 8)

Someone may ask: "Who will look after me in my old age or if I fall sick?" Listen to what Jesus says, "Therefore I say to you, do not worry about your life, what you will eat or what you will drink; nor about your body, what you will put on. Is not life more than food and the body more than clothing? Look at the birds of the air, for they neither sow nor reap nor gather into barns; yet your heavenly Father feeds them. Are you not of more value than they?" Furthermore, "Why do you worry about clothing? Consider the lilies of the field, how they grow: they neither toil nor spin; and yet I say to you that even Solomon in all his glory was not arrayed like one of these."(Matt 6: 25-28)

If you are hungry, remember the blessedness of those who are really poor and hungry and repeat these words: "Naked I came from my mother's womb, and naked shall I return there." (Job 1: 21) The Lord can never abandon a righteous man and leave him to die of starvation, "I have been young, and now am old; yet I have not seen the righteous forsaken, nor his descendants begging bread. He is ever merciful, and lends; and his descendants are blessed." (Ps. 37: 25)

Elijah was served by crows. In order to feed the prophet, the widow of Zarephath and her son were starving, yet she miraculously never ran out of flour and oil. The prophet who came asking for food was the one who provided her with food. Listen to Jacob's prayer, "Then Jacob made a vow, saying, "If God will be with me, and keep me in this way that I am going, and give me bread to eat and clothing to put on, so that I come back to my father's house in peace, then the Lord shall be my God." (Gen. 28: 20) He prayed only for the essentials, yet after 20 years, he came back to Canaan rich in children and possessions.

THE VIRTUE OF BEING MERCIFUL

Talking about charity and almsgiving takes us to the virtue of being merciful. God only cares about the motive of charity,"If a man would give for love all the wealth of his house, it would be utterly despised." (Song of Songs 8: 7) God created the entire world and is able to provide every single person with richness and possessions. However, through sublime wisdom, God allowed differences between people, to give certain people chances for doing good and acquiring the blessings of this Almsgiving service. We will find out that both the rich and the poor need each other equally.

God always wants to teach His children how to be merciful and kind to the destitute, strangers, widows and orphans. He commanded His children saying, "You shall not oppress a hired servant who is poor and needy, whether one of your brethren or one of the aliens who is in your land within your gates. Each day you shall give him his wages, and not let the sun go down on it, for he is poor and has set his heart on it; lest he cry out against you to the Lord, and it be sin to you." (Deut. 24: 14,15) Also, "You shall not pervert justice due the stranger or the fatherless, nor take a widow's garment as a pledge. But you shall remember that you were a slave in Egypt, and the Lord your God redeemed you from there; therefore I command you to do this thing." (Deut. 24: 17, 18)

God says through Isaiah the Prophet, "Learn to do good; seek justice, rebuke the oppressor, defend the fatherless, plead for the widow." (Isaiah 1: 17) In his deep words, David the Prophet says, "All my bones shall say, Lord, who is like You, delivering the poor from him who is too strong for him, yes, the poor and the needy from him who plunders him?" (Ps. 35: 10) God also says, "For I desire mercy not sacrifice, and the knowledge of God more than the burnt offerings." (Hosea 6: 6)

He also commanded the children of Israel, "Six years you shall sow your land and gather in its produce, but the seventh year you shall let it rest and lie fallow, that the poor of your people may eat; and what they leave, the beasts of the field may eat. In like manner you shall do with your vineyard and your olive grove." (Ex. 23: 10, 11) Notice in this commandment that God not only cares for His children, but also for the animals.

In the New Testament, MERCY is so clear in the personality of Jesus Himself, Who calls us to resemble our Heavenly Father, "Therefore be merciful, just as your Father also is merciful." (Luke 6: 36) He addressed the Jews saying, "But go and learn what this means, 'I desire mercy and not sacrifice'". (Matt. 9: 13) When the disciples were hungry and started plucking heads of grains and eating on a Sabbath, the Pharisees started grumbling, but He defended the disciples, giving them the example of David. They were hungry, entered the house of God and ate the showbread which was not lawful for them to eat, so then Jesus added, "But if you had known what this means, 'I desire mercy and not sacrifice,' you would not have condemned the guiltless." (Matt. 12: 1-7)

James the Apostle highlighted the virtue of mercy saying, "For judgment is without mercy to the one who has shown no mercy. Mercy triumphs over judgment." (James 2: 13)

St. John Chrysostom talked beautifully about mercy saying: "Mercy lifts us up high and lets us have favour in the eyes of God. No guards can prevent the queen from entering and talking to the king, but they will cheerfully accept her and let her enter. It is the same with a merciful person. A merciful person can stand before the throne of God without any obstacles, as the Creator loves merciful deeds. Consequently, the Lord incarnated in the shape of a human being for our salvation and gives HIS grace to those who are merciful."

He also says: "Mercy is the pinnacle of virtues and the most powerful. If you fast but have no mercy, your fasting is void. If you are a virgin resembling angels yet have no mercy, you will just stand outside the Heavenly abode." We saw the foolish virgins dismissed because they had no mercy, while the wise virgins were beautified by both: being virgins and being merciful. The wise virgins were aware of the Lord's voice: 'I desire mercy and not sacrifice.'

Who Is Eligible For Almsgiving

There are no rules for almsgiving, yet some people say we have to examine the case before giving. This issue involves two aspects: an individual aspect and a church aspect.

1. The Individual Aspect:

Lord Jesus Christ declared an important principle saying: "Give to him who asks you." (Matt. 5: 32) It is very clear that we are not supposed to examine the case of the person in need as we will be rewarded according to our love and intention for giving, "He who receives a prophet in the name of a prophet shall receive a prophet's reward. And he who receives a righteous man in the name of a righteous man shall receive a righteous man's reward. And whoever gives one of these little ones only a cup of cold water in the name of a disciple, assuredly, I say to you, he shall by no means lose his reward." (Matt. 10: 41-42)

So if you do a charitable deed to a person in need and consider him to be a prophet, a righteous or one of the Lord's disciple, you will get rewarded for this good deed, even if the person was a false prophet, a false disciple and an evil one! This allows us to serve and give to others, without judging them. We are not judges but slaves. We are called to resemble our Father in heaven, "for He makes His sun rise on the evil and on the good, and sends rain on the just and on the unjust." Assuring this, Lord Jesus ends His speech saying, "Therefore you shall be perfect, just as your Father in heaven is perfect." (Matt. 5: 45-48)

In his book "The Shepherd" Hermas wrote: "Do good deeds and give to all the needy. Do not hesitate in giving to anyone for God wants His gifts to be distributed to all. Those who take from you will give an account to God for taking. The real needy and poor will not be judged, but those who pretend to be, will be punished. Thus, he who gives is not a sinner, because he took from the Lord and simply gives to whoever deserves or doesn't deserve."

In "The Paradise of Monks" it is written that an ascetic once gave his cloak to a poor person, then, while going to the market to sell his hand production, he saw his cloak worn by a prostitute, so he grieved a lot and wept. However, God wanted to teach him a lesson and calm him down, so the angel of the Lord appeared to him and said: "Do not grieve, for the moment you gave your cloak to the poor man, its as if you gave your cloak to Christ. You are not responsible for what happened after that…"

Consequently, we don't have to investigate. However, how about if someone asks for help while you know that this person isn't in need and he will spend the money for a bad habit such as drinking? In this case, do not give to him, because when Lord Jesus said "Give to him who asks you," He didn't mean to help people going ahead with evil things!

We have to be charitable to everyone, no matter their race, religion… etc. St Paul says, "Therefore, as we have opportunity, let us do good to all, especially to those who are of the household of faith." (Gal. 6: 10)

St. John Chrysostom says: "We have to be charitable to the unbelievers as well, not only to the believers or our relatives. According to the Mosaic Law, if you see a falling donkey, you have to help it without even knowing his owner. So how much more should we look after human beings?

When the multitude followed the Lord Christ to the wilderness, He fed every one of them. Consequently, charitable deeds should be performed to all without investigation.

2. The Church Aspect:

Organisation is an important issue when it comes to the church. St. Paul the Apostle addressed the church at Corinth saying, "Now concerning the collection for the saints, as I have given orders to the churches of Galatia, so you must do also: On the first day of the week let each one of you lay something aside, storing up as he may prosper." (1 Cor. 16: 1)

Christianity urges charity but also differentiates between the needy and the lazy. St Paul declares this point saying: "For you yourselves know how you ought to follow us, for we were not disorderly among you; nor did we eat anyone's bread free of charge, but worked with labour and toil night and day, that we might not be a burden to any of you, not because we do not have authority, but to make ourselves an example of how you should follow us. For even when we were with you, we commanded you this: If anyone will not work, neither shall he eat. For we hear that there are some who walk among you in a disorderly manner, not working at all, but are busybodies. Now those who are such we command and exhort through our Lord Jesus Christ that they work in quietness and eat their own bread. But as for you, brethren, do not grow weary in doing good. And if anyone does not obey our word in this epistle, note that person and do not keep company with him, that he may be ashamed." (2 Thessalonians 3: 7 – 14)

There are many fields that require our almsgiving and tithes. They can be divided into two categories: Offerings for bodily needs such as food, medication and housing and offerings for spiritual needs such as religious lessons, preaching in remote areas, Sunday School, books and publications.

Giving money to God is a service, as some people might not be able to preach or serve in any field, yet they can serve God with their money. The Holy Bible mentions some women who used to follow Jesus,"...who provided for him from their substance." (Luke 8: 3)

Another important issue is giving of church needs; such as flour for the offering, wine, oil, incense, candles, books and altar utensils. Those who minister in poor villages (such as priests and bishops) also need tithes as they cannot perform any worldly job according to the laws of the Apostle. That is why God ordered the children of Israel to look after the Levites by offering their tithes. The Apostles in the New Testament were the same, "Do we have no right to eat and drink? Do we have no right to take along a believing wife, as do also the other apostles, the brothers of the Lord, and Cephas? Or is it only Barnabas and I who have no right to refrain from working? Who goes to war at his own expense? Who plants a vineyard and does not eat of its fruit? Or who tends a flock and does not drink of the milk of the flock?

Do I say these things as a mere man? Or does not the law say the same also? For it is written in the Law of Moses, "You shall not muzzle an ox while it treads out the grain." Is it oxen God is concerned about? Or does He say it altogether for our sakes? For our sakes, no doubt, this is written, that he who plows should plow in hope, and he who threshes in hope should be partaker of his hope. If we have sown spiritual things for you, is it a great thing if we reap your material things? If others are partakers of this right over you, are we not even more?

Nevertheless we have not used this right, but endure all things lest we hinder the gospel of Christ. Do you not know that those who minister the holy things eat of the things of the temple, and those who serve at the altar partake of the offerings of the altar? Even so the Lord has commanded that those who preach the gospel should live from the gospel." (1 Cor. 9: 4 – 14)

THE GREATNESS OF ALMSGIVING

How great and honourable is the virtue of charity. Our Lord Jesus highlighted this by saying: "He who has pity on the poor lends to the Lord and the Lord will pay back what he has given." (Prov. 19: 17) See how the Lord appears to be lending although He is the Owner of everything. The Lord tries to clarify the greatness of this virtue, and cheer the charitable ones!

Charitable deeds intercede for the believers and non-believers. It opens the doors of faith as seen with Cornelius the centurion: "… who gave alms generously to the people… about the ninth hour of the day he saw clearly in a vision an angel of God coming in and saying to him, "Cornelius!, and when he observed him, he was afraid, and said, "What is it, lord?" So he said to him, "Your prayers and your alms have come up for a memorial before God." (Acts 10) The Lord then guided him to St. Peter who baptised him and his entire household.

The great saints of God comprehended the greatness of this virtue, as Job says, "I was a father to the poor." (Job 29: 16) Solomon the Wise says, "Whoever shuts his ears to the cry of the poor will also cry himself and not be heard." (Prov. 21: 19) This was again clarified in the parable of the rich man who enjoyed a luxurious life and never considered the poor Lazarus. Finally, "Lazarus was comforted and the rich man was tormented. The rich man asked father Abraham to send Lazarus to dip the tip of his finger with water and cool his tongue." (Luke 16)

While on earth, did this rich man ever think that he would need anything from Lazarus? Did he know that being kind to Lazarus would make him enjoy father Abraham's bosom? Definitely there are many righteous people in the bosom of Abraham, but this miserable rich man despised Lazarus and never responded to his cry.

Lord Jesus Christ declared this at the parable of the Unjust Stewart. The Lord praised his wisdom by saying, "And I say to you, make friends for yourselves by unrighteous mammon, that when you fail, they may receive you into an everlasting home." (Luke 16: 9) These friends are the needy whom we approach through charitable deeds. How great is this virtue, by which we can buy an everlasting home! The Lord Jesus teaches us, "When you give a dinner or a supper, do not ask your friends, your brothers, your relatives, nor rich neighbours, lest they also invite you back, and you be repaid. But when you give a feast, invite the poor, the maimed, the lame, and the blind. And you will be blessed, because they cannot repay you; for you shall be repaid at the resurrection of the just." (Luke 14: 12 – 14)

The Lord Jesus teaches us that charitable deeds qualify us for eternal life in the Heavenly Kingdom. "Come, you blessed of My Father, inherit the kingdom prepared for you from the foundation of the world: for I was hungry and you gave Me food; I was thirsty and you gave Me drink; I was a stranger and you took Me in; I was naked and you clothed Me; I was sick and you visited Me; I was in prison and you came to Me...Assuredly, I say to you, inasmuch as you did it to one of the least of these My brethren, you did it to Me." (Matt. 25: 31 – 46)

Our Lord calls the poor and needy "My brethren." Any charitable deed done to the poor is considered being done to the Lord Himself. For this reason, charity will be our intercessor on judgment day. Beware my brethren and do not ignore charitable deeds. Love your needy and poor brethren, see Christ in them, and do not resemble the wicked ones who gave excuses for not being charitable.

St. John Chrysostom says: "A needy person stretches his hand asking for something, but God is the One Who accepts your donations."

You think that you are doing something nice when you help the poor and needy, but actually these people are giving you the chance to have a great blessing, as mentioned by St. Paul, "imploring us with much urgency that we would receive the gift and the fellowship of the ministering to the saints." (2 Cor. 8: 4)

We cannot take all our worldly riches and wealth to heaven but we can transform them into heavenly blessings by giving to the poor. We can establish for ourselves a beautiful everlasting home by building a home here for the needy. The early church fathers penned the numerous blessings and greatness of this virtue:

St. Cyprian, the Bishop and martyr who lived during the third century: The Holy Spirit talks in the Holy

Bible saying, "In mercy and truth atonement is provided for iniquity." (Prov. 16: 6) Also, "Water quenches a flaming fire, and alms resist sins." (Sirach 3: 33) The water of the Baptismal Font quenches the fire of hell, just as almsgiving and charitable deeds quench the fire of sin. In Baptism, it is done once and forever, yet the continuous act of charity provides God's mercy continuously. God emphasised this when the Pharisees targeted Christ for not washing his hands before dinner. The Lord answered, "Foolish ones! Did not He who made the outside make the inside also? But rather give alms of such things as you have; then indeed all things are clean to you." (Luke 11: 40, 41)

Archangel Rafael urges charitable deeds saying, "Prayer is good with fasting and alms, more than to lay up treasures of gold: For alms delivers from death, and the same is that which purges away sins, and makes to find mercy and life everlasting." (Tobit 12: 8, 9) This emphasises that our prayers and fasting are of less benefit for us unless they are accompanied by almsgiving.

Daniel the Prophet advised King Nebuchadnezzar, "Therefore, O king, let my advice be acceptable to you; break off your sins by being righteous, and your iniquities by showing mercy to the poor. Perhaps there may be a lengthening of your prosperity."(Daniel 4: 27)

St. Basil the Great says "Mercy will not be performed to you because you did not show mercy to others. Because you have shut the doors of your house for the needy, God will not open His doors for you. God will prevent you from the everlasting life which you seek because you did not provide food for those who asked you. You will reap what you have sowed. If you have planted bitterness or hard heartedness, you will reap bitterness, hard heartedness and horrible torments. If you have fled from mercy, it will fly away from you. If you have rejected the poor, He Who became poor , will reject you."

St. John Chrysostom says "Let's not put off our lanterns but keep them alight through charitable deeds. While still in this world, let us collect oil in our lanterns because we cannot collect it hereafter. We cannot get this oil from any other place except the hands of the needy. If you want to enter and enjoy the Heavenly Wedding, you have to collect a lot of oil; otherwise you will stay outside. It is impossible, absolutely impossible to enter the Heavenly Kingdom without charitable deeds even if you have done thousands of other good deeds."

He also comments on the Lord's words "I desire mercy and not sacrifice." "The Lord prefers mercy rather than sacrifice because sacrifices are a perishable altar and will be consumed by fire, becoming ashes and smoke, but the fruits of mercy are different." St Paul highlighted this to the Corinthians.

St. Augustine says "Don't be satisfied with prayers only, but offer your almsgiving as well. Give food to the hungry and let the palliative and homeless enter into your house. Cover a naked person and by doing this you will offer your prayers, assured that it will fly to the Lord with the two wings of fasting and almsgiving."

St. John of Assiut says "He who loves the poor resembles a person who has an intercessor at the governor's house. He who opens his doors to the needy is holding in his hands the keys to the doors of God."

SOME OF THE BLESSINGS OF ALMSGIVING

• We have seen that you can inherit the Kingdom of Heaven through your charitable deeds . The Psalmist says, "A good man deals graciously and lends; He will guide his affairs with discretion. Surely he will never be shaken; The righteous will be in everlasting remembrance... He has dispersed abroad. He has given to the poor; his righteousness endures forever; His horn will be exalted with honor." (Ps. 112: 5-9, 2 Cor. 9: 9) This issue also relates to our life here on earth, not just in eternity. We all know that the reward for charitable deeds never fades away, even after many years. Instead, it supports us during our hardships. Solomon the Wise says, "Cast your bread upon the waters, for you will find it after many days." (Ecc. 11: 1)

• Charity saves from iniquities and diseases. How wonderful are the words of David the Prophet, "Blessed is he who considers the poor; the Lord will deliver him in time of trouble. The Lord will preserve him and keep him alive, and he will be blessed on the earth. You will not deliver him to the will of the enemies. The Lord will strengthen him on his bed of illness. You will sustain him on his sickbed." (Ps. 41: 1-3)

• Charity delivers from tribulations and unwinds God's wrath. In "The Paradise of Monks" a story is written about one of the fathers who gave the last three loaves of bread he had to someone during a famine. Although he knew he would die out of hunger, he courageously fulfilled the commandment. He heard a voice from heaven announcing to him the blessing of his charitable deed.

- It delivers from sin. Joshua Son of Sirach says, "Water quenches a flaming fire, and alms resist sins." (Sirach 3: 33) Daniel the Prophet advised King Nebuchadnezzar, "break off your sins by being righteous, and your iniquities by showing mercy to the poor." (Daniel 4: 27) St John Chrysostom says: "If you are experiencing calamity, illness, grief or any other form of tribulation, give alms and thank God Who allows you to be tested through this temptation, then you will witness the flow of grace pouring on you from heaven." St. Augustine also says: "Although all our iniquities have been washed out in Baptism, we will still experience great tribulations. However prayers and almsgiving purify us from sin."

- It delivers from death as said by Tobit the righteous to his son, "For alms deliver from all sin, and from death, and will not suffer the soul to go into darkness." (Tobit 4: 11)

A STRANGE STORY FROM CONTEMPORARY HISTORY

"A charitable bank dealer in the city of Edfu in Upper Egypt was living in the fear of God and was helping 400 families. When he became old, he refused to go to church in his own car and always walked despite the long distance between his house and the church. He used to say: "How can I go to the house of God riding a car?"

At the age of 90, he was so sick and close to death. Doctors informed his family that he would die soon, and one of his members even prepared his death certificate and funeral.

However, a miracle happened. The angel of the Lord

appeared to that righteous man and said, "because of your kind heart and all the families that you are looking after, the Lord decided to extend your life for another 15 years as granted to Hezekiah the King of Judea." When his eldest son (who was around 75 years old) entered the room, he found his father sitting up on the bed, his face bright and shiny, and they all glorified the Lord and His miraculous deeds to the merciful."

St. John Chrysostom says: "If a person is sentenced to death, he would give all his riches to get saved? Don't you pay something to get delivered from eternal death?!" He who is charitable towards the needy and has mercy on them will never fall in need; neither will his descendants. "The wicked borrows and does not repay, but the righteous shows mercy and gives…I have been young, and now am old; yet I have not seen the righteous forsaken, nor his descendants begging bread. He is ever merciful and lends; and his descendants are blessed." (Ps. 37: 21 – 26) Also, "He who gives to the poor will not lack, but he who hides his eyes will have many curses." (Prov. 28: 27)

God blesses your materialistic richness. "Honour the Lord with your possessions and with the first fruits of all your increase; so your barns will be filled with plenty, and your vats will overflow with new wine." (Prov. 3: 9, 10) Also, "He who has a generous eye will be blessed, for he gives of his bread to the poor." (Prov. 22: 9)

In the Book of Malachi it is written, "Bring all the tithes into the storehouse, that there may be food in My house, and try Me now in this," Says the LORD of hosts, "If I will not open for you the windows of heaven and pour out for you such blessing that there will not be room enough to receive it." (Malachi 3: 10, 11)

"Give, and it will be given to you: good measure, pressed down, shaken together, and running over will be put into your bosom. For with the same measure that you use, it will be measured back to you."(Luke 6: 38)

A great proof of this is the widow Zarephath who fed Elijah the Prophet during the famine. The blessings didn't depart her house until it rained. Moreover, the Prophet revived her dead son. (1 Kings 17)

St. Augustine resembles the hands of the poor to a good land which gives plenty of fruits.

St. Basil the Great says: "A good deed comes back to its doer. The more water you draw from the water well, the more the water increases and becomes clear. If no water is drawn from them, they rot."

The inner happiness felt by the giver is more than enough. Philosopher Senika says: "You can never feel happy if you are living only for yourself."

There are so many blessings mentioned by the Lord to those who keep His commandments, including the virtue of charity. (Lev. 26: 3 – 13, Deut. 28: 1 – 14)

GOD ORDERS ALMSGIVING

IN THE OLD TESTAMENT

God has given clear instructions concerning the poor and needy. "Six years you shall sow your land and gather in its produce, but the seventh year you shall let it rest and lie fallow, that the poor of your people may eat; and what they leave, the beasts of the field may eat. In like manner you shall do with your vineyard and your olive grove." (Ex. 23: 10, 11) Furthermore, "If one of your brethren becomes poor, and falls into poverty among you, then you shall help him." (Lec. 25: 35)

It is also written in Deutronomy, "If there is among you a poor man of your brethren, within any of the gates in your land which the Lord your God is giving you, you shall not harden your heart nor shut your hand from your poor brother, but you shall open your hand wide to him and willingly lend him sufficient for his need, whatever he needs....You shall surely give to him, and your heart should not be grieved when you give to him, because for this thing the Lord your God will bless you in all your works and in all to which you put your hand...therefore I command you, saying, 'You shall open your hand wide to your brother, to your poor and your needy, in your land." (Deut. 15: 7 – 11)

In the same Book, "When you reap your harvest in your field, and forget a sheaf in the field, you shall not go back to get it; it shall be for the stranger, the fatherless, and the widow, that the Lord your God may bless you in all the work of your hands. When you beat your olive trees, you shall not go over the boughs again; it shall be for the stranger, the fatherless, and the widow. When you gather the grapes of your vineyard, you shall not glean it afterward; it shall be for the stranger, the fatherless, and the widow." (Deut. 24: 19 – 21)

The Lord talked about Acceptable fasting through Isaiah the Prophet saying, "Is it not to share your bread with the hungry, and that you bring to your house the poor who are cast out. When you see the naked, that you cover him, and not hide yourself from your own flesh? Then your light shall break forth like the morning, your healing shall spring forth speedily, and your righteousness shall go before you; The glory of the Lord shall be your rear guard. Then you shall call, and the Lord will answer; You shall cry, and He will say, 'Here I am.'(Isaiah 58: 7-9)

Tobit advised his son saying, "Give alms out of your substance, and turn not away your face from any poor person: for so it shall come to pass that the face of the Lord shall not be turned from you. According to your ability, be merciful. For thus you store up to yourself a good reward for the day of necessity. For alms deliver from all sin, and from death, and will not suffer the soul to go into darkness. Alms shall be a great confidence before the most high God, to all them that give it." (Tobit 4: 7 – 12)

The Lord promised strict punishments to those who neglect the poor. One of the reasons for burning Sodom was, "Look, this was the iniquity of your sister Sodom: She and her daughter had pride, fullness of food, and abundance of idleness; neither did she strengthen the hand of the poor and needy." (Ez. 16: 49)

The Lord also said through Moses the prophet, "You shall not oppress a hired servant who is poor and needy, whether one of your brethren or one of the aliens who is in your land within your gates. Each day you shall give him his wages, and not let the sun go down on it, for he is poor and has set his heart on it; lest he cry out against you to the Lord, and it be sin to you." (Deut. 24: 14, 15)

David the prophet says, "I know that the Lord will maintain the cause of the afflicted and the justice for the poor." (Ps. 140: 12) Furthermore, "For He shall regard the prayer of the destitute, and shall not despise their prayers." (Ps. 102: 17)

Evenmore, out of His great compassion for the poor, the Lord made Himself a father to the orphans and a judge to the widows. He looks after them and avenges those who are unjust towards them, as they have no other to care for them, "A Father of the fatherless, a defender of the widows, is God in His Holy habitation." (Ps. 68: 5) Also, "Lord, You have heard the desire of the humble; You will prepare their heart; You will cause Your ear to hear, to do justice to the fatherless and the oppressed, that the man of the earth may oppress no more." (Ps. 10: 17, 18)

Joshua Son of Sirach approved the same, "In judging, be merciful to the fatherless as a father, and as a husband to their mother, and you shall be as the obedient son of the most High, and he will have mercy on you more than a mother."(Sirach 4: 10)

When John the Baptist rebuked the crowd who came to get baptised by him, he urged them to bear fruits worthy of repentance. They asked him what were these fruits, and he answered, "Then he said to the multitudes that came out to be baptized by him, "Brood of vipers! Who warned you to flee from the wrath to come? Therefore bear fruits worthy of repentance…. therefore every tree which does not bear good fruit is cut down and thrown into the fire." So the people asked him, saying, "What shall we do then?" He answered and said to them, "He who has two tunics, let him give to him who has none; and he who has food, let him do likewise."(Luke 3: 7‑ 11)

IN THE NEW TESTAMENT

The Lord of glory talks a lot about charitable deeds and love for the poor, "Sell what you have and give alms; provide yourselves money bags which do not grow old, a treasure in the heavens that does not fail, where no thief approaches nor moth destroys. For where your treasure is, there your heart will be also."(Luke 12: 33, 34) Also, "But rather give alms of such things as you have; then indeed all things are clean to you." (Luke 11: 41) Moreover, "But love your enemies, do good, and lend, hoping for nothing in return; and your reward will be great, and you will be sons of the Most High. For He is kind to the unthankful and evil. Therefore be merciful, just as your Father also is merciful." (Luke 6: 35, 36)

After the Lord mentioned the parable of the rich man whose ground yielded plentifully, He described the man as a fool, "So is he who lays up treasure for himself, and is not rich toward God." (Luke 12: 16 – 21)

In the parable of the rich man and Lazarus, which we mentioned earlier, the Lord explained the sin of this rich man, "There was a certain rich man who was clothed in purple and fine linen and fared sumptuously every day." He always ignored Lazarus the poor man who was, "…full of sores, who was laid at his gate, desiring to be fed with the crumbs which fell from the rich man's table." (Luke 16: 19 – 21)

The teachings of the Lord Jesus about charity were reflected on His disciples and apostles, and this was clear in their writings. St Paul says in his farewell sermon to the priests of Ephesus, "…and remember the words of the Lord Jesus that He said 'It is more blessed to give than to receive.'" (Acts 20: 35) He also wrote to Timothy, "Command those who are rich in this present age not to be haughty, nor to trust in uncertain riches but in the living God, who gives us richly all things to enjoy. Let them do good, that they be rich in good works, ready to give, willing to share, storing up for themselves a good foundation for the time to come, that they may lay hold on eternal life." (1 Tim. 6: 17 – 19)

Closing his Epistle to the Hebrews, he says: "Let brotherly love continue. Do not forget to entertain strangers, for by so doing some have unwittingly entertained angels. Remember the prisoners as if chained with them—those who are mistreated—since you yourselves are in the body also." (Heb. 13: 1-5) There is no doubt that brotherly love is shown through positive deeds, such as charitable works. He also urges the believers to share with those who are mistreated. The following verse stresses the aforementioned, "Let your conduct be without covetousness."

St. James the Apostle, in beautiful words, talks about charitable deeds. He summarised the whole issue in these words, "Pure and undefiled religion before God and the

Father is this: to visit orphans and widows in their trouble, and to keep oneself unspotted from the world." (James 1: 27) Notice that he mentioned charitable deeds before keeping oneself unspotted from the world!

CHARITY IN THE EARLY CHURCH

Faith in the Lord Jesus Christ, through the Holy Spirit, made the believers feel they have one heart and one soul; "Now the multitude of those who believed were of one heart and one soul; neither did anyone say that any of the things he possessed was his own, but they had all things in common."(Acts 4: 32)

St. Luke explained the state of the early church by saying, "And with great power the apostles gave witness to the resurrection of the Lord Jesus. And great grace was upon them all. Nor was there anyone among them who lacked; for all who were possessors of lands or houses sold them, and brought the proceeds of the things that were sold, and laid them at the apostles' feet; and they distributed to each as anyone had need." (Acts 4: 33- 35);(Acts 2: 44, 45)

When the numbers of believers were multiplying and there were lots of donations and gifts, the disciples appointed some deacons to look after this mission, so that they might not neglect the prayers and the ministry of the word. So giving was a main issue in the church since the very beginning, and nobody could ignore the great impact that charitable deeds had on the establishment of the early church.

During his missionary trips, St. Paul cared strongly about serving the poor,"They desired only that we should remember the poor, the very thing which I also was eager to do." (Gal. 2: 10) In Caeserea where St Paul was arrested, he defended himself before the governor saying, "Now after many years I came to bring alms and offerings to my nation." (Acts 24: 17) In his epistle to the Hebrews, after urging them to pray and praise, he reminded them of charitable deeds by saying, "But do not forget to do good and to share, for with such sacrifices God is well pleased." (Heb. 13: 16) and(Phil. 4: 17 – 19)

WHO ARE WE SUPPOSED TO GIVE

Everyone is expected to give, without discrimination, including priests who accept almsgiving from the congregation. St Paul says, "Therefore, as we have opportunity, let us do good to all." (Gal. 6: 10)

When talking about the Christians in Macedonia, St Paul mentions: "Moreover, brethren, we make known to you the grace of God bestowed on the churches of Macedonia: that in a great trial of affliction the abundance of their joy and their deep poverty abounded in the riches of their liberality. For I bear witness that according to their ability, yes, and beyond their ability…" (2Cor. 8: 1- 3) For though they were extremely poor, they gave genorously.

One of the greatest stories in the Bible about Almsgiving is the widow who gave two mites. The Lord Jesus praised her saying, "All these people gave their gifts out of their wealth; but she out of her poverty put in all she had to live on." (Luke 21: 1-4)

St John Chrysostom says: "Talking about charity my brethren includes also the poor and needy, not only the rich and wealthy. There is great benefit and salvation for everyone in charitable deeds. Even if someone is a beggar and gives, it will benefit him greatly. There is no one who is so poor that he can not even give two mites."

How to Offer Almsgiving

When Lord Jesus sat opposite the treasury, He was watching "how people put money into the treasury." (Mark 12: 41) God doesn't care about the quantity. He cares about our attitude while offering. Cain and Abel both offered to God, but "the Lord respected Abel and his offering, but He did not respect Cain and his offering." (Gen. 4: 4,5) Now…how do we offer?

1. Paying for a Debt:

When we offer, we should not feel that we are doing God a favour, but we have to be aware that we are offering some of what He had already given us. After he had gathered a lot of gold and silver to build the house of the Lord, David said, "For all things come from You, and of Your own we have given You." (1 Chr. 29: 14) So, we have to remember that we owe the Lord a great debt which we have to give back. He gave us everything, so really we are returning what is His.

God's gifts are not only material, but extend to the greatest gift which is His sublime salvation, "knowing that you were not redeemed with corruptible things, like silver or gold, from your aimless conduct received by tradition from your fathers, but with the precious blood of Christ, as of a lamb without blemish and without spot." (1 Peter 1: 18, 19)

When St Paul talked about the offerings of the Macedonians, he attracted their attention to God's greatest gift, "For you know the grace of our Lord Jesus Christ, that though He was rich, yet for your sakes He became poor, that you through His poverty might become rich." (2 Cor. 8, 9) We should accompany offerings to God with prayer, so that they can be accepted. If a poor person accepts your offerings, he has done a great favour for you.

St. Paul expressed this by saying, "For it pleased those from Macedonia and Achaia to make a certain contribution for the poor among the saints who are in Jerusalem...Now I beg you, brethren, through the Lord Jesus Christ, and through the love of the Spirit, that you strive together with me in prayers to God for me, that I may be delivered from those in Judea who do not believe, and that my service for Jerusalem may be acceptable to the saints." (Romans 15: 27 – 31)

2. In Love:

In every virtue, law or practice, love is like the spirit for the body. If the spirit and body are separated, the body becomes a dead corpse. It is the same case with any virtue void of love, as it will be rejected by God. Christianity is a sublime religion which makes us share the feelings of others, "rejoicing with those who rejoice and weeping with those who weep." It is also said that our God, "sympathises with our weaknesses..." (Heb. 4: 15)

He who has no brotherly love proves that he is not a disciple of the Lord, as the Lord says: 'By this all will know that you are My disciples, if you have love for one another."(John 13: 35) Also, "Whoever has this world's goods, and sees his brother in need, and shuts up his heart from him, how does the love of God abide in him? My little children, let us not love in word or in tongue, but in deed and in truth." (1 John 3: 17, 18)

We have to resemble our Heavenly Father who made tunics of skin, and clothed Adam and Eve after they became naked of the clothes of grace. (Gen. 3: 21] St Paul assured this by saying: "And though I bestow all my goods to feed the poor, and though I give my body to be burned, but have not love, it profits me nothing." (1 Cor. 13: 3)

The Lord allowed social differences between His children so they can practise sublime virtues, and without doubt, love is the summit of all virtues. When I love my brethren the poor and needy, I consider them my brothers and sisters. The Apostle calls this 'The bond of perfection.' It is crystal clear that if I am doing my offerings without love, they are completely rejected, "If a man would give for love all the wealth of his house, it would be utterly despised." (Song of Songs 8: 7)

3. In Free Will:

Giving shouldn't be a result of shyness or consistent demanding, but of free will. "So let each one give as he purposes in his heart, not grudgingly or of necessity; for God loves a cheerful giver." (2 Cor. 9: 7)

Talking about the Macedonians St. Paul writes, "For I bear witness that according to their ability, yes, and beyond their ability, they were freely willing, imploring us with much urgency that we would receive the gift and the fellowship of the ministering to the saints." (2 Cor. 8: 3)

4. In Self-Denial:

The principle of self-denial was highly stressed by the Lord Jesus. St Paul urged self-denial to the Colossians, "And whatever you do, do it heartily, as to the Lord and not to men, knowing that from the Lord you will receive the reward of the inheritance; for you serve the Lord Christ." (Col. 3: 23, 24)

As for almsgiving and charitable deeds the Lord Jesus says: "Take heed that you do not do your charitable deeds before men, to be seen by them. Otherwise you have no reward from your Father in heaven. Therefore, when you do a charitable deed, do not sound a trumpet before you as the hypocrites do in the synagogues and in the streets, that they may have glory from men. Assuredly, I say to you, they have their reward. But when you do a charitable deed, do not let your left hand know what your right hand is doing, that your charitable deed may be in secret; and your Father who sees in secret will Himself reward you openly." (Matt. 6: 1 – 4)

The Lord's commandment "Do not let your left hand know what your right hand is doing" reminds us of the Lord's desire for self- denial. If people see us without our intention of being seen, it does not affect God's acceptance of our offerings.

5. Generously to the best of our ability:

As children of God, we have to resemble our Heavenly Father, "who gives to all liberally and without reproach." (James 1: 5) The Lord ordered His children from the beginning, "Then you shall keep the Feast of Weeks to the Lord your God with the tribute of a freewill offering from your hand, which you shall give as the Lord your God blesses you." (Deut. 16: 10)

St. Paul also talks about it, "Command those who are rich in this present age not to be haughty, nor to trust in uncertain riches but in the living God, who gives us richly all things to enjoy. Let them do good, that they be rich in good works, ready to give, willing to share..." (1 Tim. 6: 17, 18) St Paul also wrote to the Corinthians about the believers in Macedonia, saying; "Moreover, brethren, we make known to you the grace of God bestowed on the churches of Macedonia: that in a great trial of affliction the abundance of their joy and their deep poverty abounded in the riches of their liberality. For I bear witness that according to their ability, yes, and beyond their ability, they were freely willing, imploring us with much urgency that we would receive the gift and the fellowship of the ministering to the saints. And not only as we had hoped, but they first gave themselves to the Lord, and then to us by the will of God." (2 Cor. 8: 1 – 5)

Here, the Apostle reveals the secret of this abundance, "They first gave themselves to the Lord!" Would a person who gave himself totally to the Lord be stingy with other trifle issues such as money, time, and effort? Some people might give many things openly, but the heart from inside is not upright or consecrated to the Lord. A good example is Ananias and Sapphira as mentioned in the book of Acts Chapter 5.

Generosity was the real quality of the early church. We notice that St. Paul affirms, "But this I say: He who sows sparingly will also reap sparingly, and he who sows bountifully will also reap bountifully." (2 Cor. 9: 6)

St Cyprian, the Bishop and Martyr, commenting on the story of the widow and her two mites says: "Blessed is this woman, who deserved to be praised by the Great Judge even before Judgment Day! The needy woman was rich in her deeds as she gave when she really needed to take."

6. In Joy and Happiness:

Happiness is a proof of good intention and brotherly love towards the needy, as St Paul says: "So let each one give as he purposes in his heart, not grudgingly or of necessity; for God loves a cheerful giver." (2 Cor. 9: 7)

St John Chrysostom comments on our father Abraham hosting the three men: "I wonder about Abraham the father of fathers. Although he had 318 servants, yet he personally attended to the three men. Although he was an old skinny man, he hurried to the cattle and took the calf. Do not be ashamed to personally serve the needy if you are a rich one. The Lord Jesus Christ, your Creator, was not shy to take the offerings of the needy. How come you are ashamed to stretch your arm and give Him a little of your food or possessions? Our hands will be blessed when we serve the poor and needy. Then when we lift our hands for prayer, the Creator will look at us, have mercy on us and always respond to our prayer."

Some people rebuke the poor person after giving him. Regarding this, St Paul says: "But you have dishonoured the poor man." (James 6: 2)

St John Chrysostom says: "A merciful person is the great, kind and generous one, who does charitable deeds cheerfully. His good heart makes him believe he is taking not giving, thus he is the winner."

7. From a Legal Profit:

The Church Laws institute not to accept offerings from evil ones and non-believers. If the Church is forced to accept them, they should be spent in firewood or coal for burning, as money gained from a sinful source should be burnt. It is a great insult to offer money from an illegal profit, or money gathered from a sin like adultery.

The Lord says through Malachi the Prophet: "Yet you say, 'In what way have we despised Your name?'... and when you offer the blind as a sacrifice, is it not evil? And when you offer the lame and sick, is it not evil? Offer it then to your governor! Would he be pleased with you? Would he accept you favourably?" Says the Lord of hosts... I have no pleasure in you," says the Lord of hosts, "Nor will I accept an offering from your hands." (Malachi 1: 6- 10)

St John Chrysostom emphasises that charity is better than fasting and prayer. He says: "It should be from legal profit and hard work, not as a result of greed and violence. Impure offerings upset the Lord and never please Him. So, let us be very cautious lest we should insult Him instead of serving Him. Cain was punished severely because he didn't offer his best. How will it be with us if we offer something gathered illegally or through greed and violence?"

TITHES

Giving tithes was practiced by the children of God even before the Mosaic Law. We read about Abraham, who lived before Moses, while coming back from the defeat of Chedorlaomer, that he gave Melchizedek the High Priest of God great tithes. Melchizedek accepted the tithes and blessed Abraham. (Gen. 14: 20) It is worth noticing that Abraham offered the tithes to Melchizedek because he was the Priest of God Most High and not because of their friendship.

St. Paul pointed to this incident in his epistle to the Hebrews, intending to prove the virtue of Melchizedek's priesthood, "For this Melchizedek, king of Salem, priest of the Most High God, who met Abraham returning from the slaughter of the kings and blessed him, to whom also Abraham gave a tenth part of all, first being translated "king of righteousness," and then also king of Salem, meaning "king of peace," without father, without mother, without genealogy, having neither beginning of days nor end of life, but made like the Son of God, remains a priest continually.

Now consider how great this man was, to whom even the patriarch Abraham gave a tenth of the spoils. And indeed those who are of the sons of Levi, who receive the priesthood, have a commandment to receive tithes from the people according to the law, that is, from their brethren, though they have come from the loins of Abraham; but he whose genealogy is not derived from them received tithes from Abraham and blessed him who had the promises. Now beyond all contradiction the lesser is blessed by the better. Here mortal men receive tithes, but there he receives them, of whom it is witnessed that he lives. Even Levi, who receives tithes, paid tithes through Abraham, so to speak, for he was still in the loins of his father when Melchizedek met him." (Heb. 7: 1-10)

After Jacob saw the ladder joining earth to heaven, he

made a vow saying: "If God will be with me, and keep me in this way that I am going, and give me bread to eat and clothing to put on, so that I come back to my father's house in peace, then the LORD shall be my God. And this stone which I have set as a pillar shall be God's house, and of all that You give me I will surely give a tenth to You." (Gen. 28: 20 – 22)

THE MOSAIC LAW

Tithes were mentioned in the commandments given to Moses. The Lord ordered His people to give tithes of all their income, "You shall truly tithe all the increase of your grain that the field produces year by year. And you shall eat before the Lord your God, in the place where He chooses to make His name abide, the tithe of your grain and your new wine and your oil, of the firstborn of your herds and your flocks, that you may learn to fear the Lord your God always." (Deut. 14: 22, 23)

Tithes in this form was a kind of honouring the Lord, and an announcement from the children of Israel that the Lord is the Owner of the entire land, and the Giver of all its fruits and grains. Thus, they had to offer thanksgiving and honour to the Lord because of His abundant riches to them.

Solomon the Wise says, "Honor the Lord with your possessions, and with the firstfruits of all your increase, so your barns will be filled with plenty, and your vats will overflow with new wine." (Prov.3: 9, 10) There are many forms of tithes mentioned in the Old Testament:

1- The first kind of the tithes:

"And all the tithe of the land, whether of the seed of the land or of the fruit of the tree, is the Lord's. It is holy to the Lord." (Lev. 27: 30) This tithe could not be redeemed or exchanged, if so the commandement was, "If a man wants at all to redeem any of his tithes, he shall add one-fifth to it, and concerning the tithe of the herd or the flock, of whatever passes under the rod, the tenth one shall be holy to the Lord. He shall not inquire whether it is good or bad, nor shall he exchange it; and if he exchanges it at all, then both it and the one exchanged for it shall be holy; it shall not be redeemed." (Lev. 27: 31 – 33)

It could not be used for any other purpose because it was solely dedicated to the Lord. This part of the tithes was given to the children of Levi, "Then the Lord said to Aaron: "You shall have no inheritance in their land, nor shall you have any portion among them; I am your portion and your inheritance among the children of Israel. Tithes for Support of the Levites "Behold, I have given the children of Levi all the tithes in Israel as an inheritance in return for the work which they perform, the work of the tabernacle of meeting…For the tithes of the children of Israel, which they offer up as a heave offering to the Lord, I have given to the Levites as an inheritance; therefore I have said to them, 'Among the children of Israel they shall have no inheritance." (Num. 18: 20 – 21)

2- Another kind of tithes related to celebrations and feasts which could be redeemed or exchanged

"You shall truly tithe all the increase of your grain that the field produces year by year. And you shall eat before the Lord your God, in the place where He chooses to make His name abide, the tithe of your grain and your new wine and your oil, of the firstborn of your herds and your flocks, that you may learn to fear the Lord your God always. But if the journey is too long for you, so that you are not able to carry the tithe, or if the place where the Lord your God chooses to put His name is too far from you, when the Lord your God has blessed you, then you shall exchange it for money, take the money in your hand, and go to the place which the Lord your God chooses. And you shall spend that money for whatever your heart desires: for oxen or sheep, for wine or similar drink, for whatever your heart desires; you shall eat there before the Lord your God, and you shall rejoice, you and your household. You shall not forsake the Levite who is within your gates, for he has no part nor inheritance with you." (Deut. 14: 22 – 27)

3- Tithes for the poor, needy and strangers once every three years.

"At the end of every third year you shall bring out the tithe of your produce of that year and store it up within your gates. And the Levite, because he has no portion nor inheritance with you, and the stranger and the fatherless and the widow who are within your gates, may come and eat and be satisfied, that the Lord your God may bless you in all the work of your hand which you do." (Deut. 28: 28, 29)

4- Tithes are also mentioned for the house of God (Deut. 12: 5, 6 and Nehemiah 10: 25, 37, 38 and 13: 12, Also Amos 4: 4 and Malachi 3: 10)

So, when the Lord organised worship for the Jews, one of the rules was to give the tithes to the Lord, "Bring all the tithes into the storehouse (i.e. the storehouse of the Lord's house), that there may be food in My house, (i.e. food for the priests and Levites and the servants of the house of God, and whoever comes in need. (Malachi 3: 10) We also read in Nehemiah that he asked for the tithes, offerings, vows and all other donations when people were reluctant to do so, "So I contended with the rulers and said 'Why is the house of the Lord forsaken?" (Neh. 13: 11)

In addition to the commandments, we read about promises and blessings to His children. Amongst all of them, the strongest is promised to those who give their tithes. In this commandment, the Lord puts Himself in the position of being tested and tried, "Bring all the tithes into the storehouse….and try Me now in this,' says the Lord of hosts. "If I will not open for you the windows of heaven and pour out for you such blessing, that there will not be room enough to receive it." (Malachi 3: 10) It is written, "You shall not tempt the Lord your God," (Deut. 6: 16 and Matt. 4: 7) yet in this particular issue, the Lord says, "Try Me."

Do we still doubt God's truthfulness? Do we need to tempt or test Him? What is meant by 'tempt' is not to prove His honesty of promises, but to prove our belief in His promises. "If I will not open for you the windows of heaven and pour out for you such blessing, that there will not be room enough to receive it." What about the windows of heaven which flooded the entire world during the time of Noah? How would it be like if the windows of heaven pour blessings and goodness!

The Lord holds many promises to those who give their tithes, " And I will rebuke the devourer for your sakes, so that he will not destroy the fruit of your ground, nor shall the vine fail to bear fruit for you in the field," says the Lord of hosts; And all nations will call you blessed, for you will be a delightful land," Says the Lord of hosts." (Malachi 3: 11, 12)

On the other hand, those who refrain from giving tithes are cursed and robbers. In amazement the Lord says, " Will a man rob God? Yet you have robbed Me! But you say, 'In what way have we robbed You?' In tithes and offerings. You are cursed with a curse, for you have robbed Me, even this whole nation." (Mal. 3: 8, 9)

The New Testament:

The Lord Jesus Christ announced "Do not think that I came to destroy the Law or the Prophets. I did not come to destroy but to fulfill." (Matt. 5: 17) The commandment of tithes was not destroyed in the New Testament but was left for thanksgiving and honour to the Lord. The Lord Jesus says, "Woe to you, scribes and Pharisees, hypocrites! For you pay tithe of mint and anise and cummin, and have neglected the weightier matters of the law: justice and mercy and faith. These you ought to have done, without leaving the others undone. " (Matt. 23: 23 and Luke 11: 32)

That was concerning tithes generally. But the Lord Jesus announced, "For I say to you, that unless your righteousness exceeds the righteousness of the scribes and Pharisees, you will by no means enter the kingdom of heaven." (Matt. 5: 20)

The Scribes and Pharisees used to be proud of giving tithes. The Lord Jesus spoke about the parable between the Pharisee and tax collector in Luke 18. St Luke started this parable by saying, "Also He spoke this parable to some who trusted in themselves that they were righteous, and despised others."

Therefore, in the New Testament, tithes were the minimum one could give, and the utmost level was to "..sell what you have and give alms." (Luke 12: 33) Also, "But rather give alms of such things as you have; then indeed all things are clean to you." (Luke 11: 41)

Actually, we do not read about a fixed system of almsgiving in the New Testament. It was optional and voluntary, and this is clear in the story of Ananias and Sapphira, "But Peter said, "Ananias, why has Satan filled your heart to lie to the Holy Spirit and keep back part of the price of the land for yourself? While it remained, was it not your own? And after it was sold, was it not in your own control? Why have you conceived this thing in your heart? You have not lied to men but to God."(Acts 5: 3, 4) The commitment comes from one's inner feelings, when St. Paul talked to the Corinthians saying, "Now concerning the collection for the saints, as I have given orders to the churches of Galatia, so you must do also: On the first day of the week let each one of you lay something aside, storing up as he may prosper, that there be no collections when I come. And when I come, whomever you approve by your letters I will send to bear your gift to Jerusalem. But if it is fitting that I go also, they will go with me." (1 Cor. 16: 1 – 3) The early church applied this blessed principle, "….. and remember the words of the Lord Jesus, that He said, 'It is more blessed to give than to receive.'"(Acts 2: 35)

Sayings of the Church Fathers about almsgiving and tithes:

First Century:

Many people in the first centuries sold their possessions and offered them to the Apostles, who distributed them to the needy, "Now the multitude of those who believed were of one heart and one soul; neither did anyone say that any of the things he possessed was his own, but they had all things in common. And with great power the apostles gave witness to the resurrection of the Lord Jesus. And great grace was upon them all. Nor was there anyone among them who lacked; for all who were possessors of lands or houses sold them, and brought the proceeds of the things that were sold, and laid them at the apostles' feet; and they distributed to each as anyone had need." (Acts 4: 32 – 35) Also"Then the disciples, each according to his ability, determined to send relief to the brethren dwelling in Judea" (Acts 11: 29)

Addressing the Galatians and Corinthians, the Apostle recommended that each one should pay 'according to his ability.' (1Cor. 16: 1 – 2)

Second Century:

The Christian spirit of love, giving and sharing was still prevailing. St. Ireanous says: "Our Lord came to extend the Mosaic Law, He replaced orders with principles, thus, instead of "do not commit adultery," it is "do not covet", instead of "do not kill," it is "do not get angry," and instead of "pay the tithes," a person can sell all his possessions and give to the poor. In such, Christ removed the chains of slavery."

Again, St. Ireanous compares the slavery of the Mosaic Law to the freedom and sonship of Christians: "For this reason, while the Jews considered the tithes of their possessions to belong to God, those who were liberated, served the Lord with all their possessions, in joy and freedom, not giving less, but according to great hope."

Third Century:

Origen said the offering of firstfruits and tithes are not a duty for Christians, but a minimum offering which they have to add to, "Woe to you, scribes and Pharisees, hypocrites! For you pay tithe of mint and anise and cummin, and have neglected the weightier matters of the law: justice and mercy and faith. These you ought to have done, without leaving the others undone. " (Matt. 23: 23)

St. Origen says: "If you claim that the Lord Jesus was just addressing the Pharisees and not the disciples; then listen to what He says to His disciples; "For I say to you, that unless your righteousness exceeds the righteousness of the scribes and Pharisees, you will by no means enter the kingdom of heaven." (Matt. 5: 20). Thus, He wanted the disciples to do more than what the Pharisees were doing, otherwise, how would our righteousness exceeds that of the Scribes and Pharisees?"

St Cyprian grieved for the shortage in almsgiving, saying: "In early Christianity they used to sell houses and possessions, while now we are not even giving the tithes. While the Lord orders us to sell, we are rather buying and getting wealthier."

Fourth Century:

St. Ambrose says in his 34th Sermon: "God kept one tenth for Himself, and no one has the right to take God's share for himself. He gave you nine shares and just kept for Himself one tenth. If you don't give what is His, He will take away the other nine shares." He also said: "A good Christian gives his tithes yearly to be given to the poor."

Fifth Century:

St. Ironimus explains Malachi Chapter Three saying: "The church congregation have always followed the almsgiving of tithes and firstfuits given to the priests and Levites. They were advised to sell what they have, give to the poor and follow the Saviour. If we are not ready to do this, at least let us resemble the early Jewish teachings and give a part to the poor, as well as giving the priests and Levites their honour and respect. If anyone doesn't accept these teachings, then he is a criminal, robbing and deceiving the Lord."

St. Augustine interpreted Psalm 146 by saying: "Assign something or a certain percentage for God. Are you giving the tithes? Give your tithes no matter how little they are." In his 48th Sermon he talked about the increased taxes of the time and people's reluctance in giving God his share. He said: "Our ancestors were so rich because they regularly gave tithes and taxes to Caesar. Now, the contrary is happening. As people stop giving to God, the drainage of money increases. We have to give our almsgiving according to what is mentioned in the Book of Tobit 4: 8, "If you have abundance give alms accordingly: if you have but a little, be not afraid to give according to that little.""

Some Objections Against Almsgiving

Some people might refrain from giving their tithes, although this is the minimum offering. They claim that they have many expenses and are following an incorrect prioritisation. They spend on their house needs first before they think of the church. Others might refrain from giving their tithes to save money for the future, or because life is hard and unsecure. While a third group will not even think of giving tithes in the first place, and if they do, they just give a trifle amount, far away from their income.

Some people do not believe in almsgiving, claiming that all the poor and needy people are pretending, and they are really rich and are not in need at all. There are so many more reasons and claims for not giving tithes and offerings...

First Objection: (The high cost of living and one's many responsibilities)

If God has promised that a cup of cold water will be rewarded, how about he who feeds and clothes the Lord when he gives the hungry and the naked. The real problem of this modern time is lack of faith. People just love with their minds without giving a chance for faith to work within themselves.

These people use their calculator to count their expenditure, and then nothing is left for God. This is a grieve mistake because if they give God, it is from their leftovers. They are not giving God out of their need. The

Lord praised the two mite widow, "for they all put in out of their abundance, but she out of her poverty put in all that she had, her whole livelihood."(Mark 12: 44)

We know that the Lord Jesus is the Alpha and the Omega, the Beginning and the End. We have to act accordingly, and give God the priority in every aspect of our lives.

We have to remember Elijah's words to the widow of Zarephath, "And when he came to the gate of the city, indeed a widow was there gathering sticks. And he called to her and said, "Please bring me a little water in a cup, that I may drink." And as she was going to get it, he called to her and said, "Please bring me a morsel of bread in your hand." So she said, "As the Lord your God lives, I do not have bread, only a handful of flour in a bin, and a little oil in a jar; and see, I am gathering a couple of sticks that I may go in and prepare it for myself and my son, that we may eat it, and die." And Elijah said to her, "Do not fear; go and do as you have said, but make me a small cake from it first, and bring it to me; and afterward make some for yourself and your son." (1Kings 17: 11 – 16) In this case, the Lord came first, then the man of God, and last the widow and her son. Consequently, this is the mystery of the blessing, "The bin of flour was not used up, nor did the jar of oil run dry, according to the word of the Lord which He spoke by Elijah."

Elijah the Prophet was not selfish when he asked for bread for himself first, but he was sure of God's blessings which will fall upon this widow. The widow's hosting and honouring to Elijah was not presented to him, it was directed to the Lord. Yet, Elijah was the Lord's servant and

"He who honours you honours Me."

Second Objection: (Saving)

Here, we can divide the issue of "Saving" into two main kinds:

a) Saving just for the sake of collecting money, where a person saves the excess of his expenditure, without targeting the money saved for a specific reason. Christianity considers this 'the love of money', on which the Lord says: "Do not lay up for yourselves treasures on earth."

b) A person saves an amount of money to be spent in buying something or for an important basic issue. Although it looks like this person is saving money, we know where this money is going because there is an important aim. This is not considered love of money. For example, a father who has to pay fees for his childrens' education, must save money at the beginning of each year, otherwise, his children will be delayed in their education. Similarly, if one is saving up for their daughter's wedding. However, this should be done while maintaining ones tithes and almsgiving.

Our Lord Jesus Christ commands us, "Therefore do not worry about tomorrow, for tomorrow will worry about its own things. Sufficient for the day is its own trouble." (Matt. 6: 34)

St. Cyprian the Bishop and Martyr says: "Give the Lord your wealth which you are keeping for inheritance, make him the guardian for your children. He is the great protector who will protect them against all the evils of the entire world."

Third Objection (Doubting the sincerity of those in need)

We addressed this issue when we talked about whom to give almsgiving.

EXAMPLES OF GENEROUS ALMSGIVING PERSONALITIES

The Holy Bible mentions many personalities who loved the Lord, and hence they were merciful. Job the Righteous was "...the greatest of all the people of the East" (Job 1: 3), yet he was merciful, saying, "Because I delivered the poor who cried out, the fatherless and the one who had no helper. The blessing of a perishing man came upon me, and I caused the widow's heart to sing for joy. I put on righteousness, and it clothed me; My justice was like a robe and a turban. I was eyes to the blind, and I was feet to the lame. I was a father to the poor, and I searched out the case that I did not know." (Job 29: 12 – 16)

Also, "If I have kept the poor from their desire, or caused the eyes of the widow to fail, or eaten my morsel by myself, so that the fatherless could not eat of it...If I have seen anyone perish for lack of clothing,Or any poor man without covering...Then let my arm fall from my shoulder, let my arm be torn from the socket." (Job 31: 16 – 22)

The church's history is full of merciful personalities. We will mention a few examples.

<u>St. Peter the Worshipper:</u>

He started his career as a heart-hearted tax-collector, extremely miser to the extent that people used to call him the 'unmerciful'. One day, a poor man came asking for a donation, but he became more persistent when Peter just ignored him. In the meanwhile, his servant came carrying fresh baked bread, so Peter, to get rid of the poor man, threw a loaf of bread to him intending to hit him with the loaf and not out of mercy or any charitable deed. That night in a dream, Peter saw himself standing before the Lord on Judgment Day, the angels couldn't find any good deed except the loaf of bread with which he hit the poor man. He woke up trembling, and was too anxious about the dream, blaming himself for his harshness and cruelty. Immediately, he distributed all his wealth to the needy and poor, and when he couldn't find anything else to give, he sold his robe and gave its money to the poor. It is said that later he sold himself as a slave and also gave this money to the poor.

When he became renowned for his charity and virtues, he headed to the wilderness of Scetis where he spent the rest of his life in strict worship and asceticism. He deserved to know the date of his departrue from this vain world. The church commemorates him on the 25th of the Coptic month of Tubah.

Contour Ibrahim El Gohary:

He was in the position of a Prime Minister during the Turkish and Memluk's rule in Egypt, yet he was a very humble and charitable person. It is mentioned that he used to divide his income into three portions: one third for books script and printing and two thirds for the poor and needy, and for refurbishing and renovating the old churches and monasteries. He was fulfilling his Master's command "Give to everyone who asks of you. And from him who takes away your goods, do not ask them back." Luke 6: 30) He never differentiated between a Muslim or Christian.

As he was renowned for his extreme generosity and charitable deeds, a poor person tried to trick him by asking Mr. Ibrahim for a donation, to which he gave him some money. The man asked him again on another street, yet he gave him again. The man went eighteen times on that day, while Ibrahim never grumbed or rebuked the man. Finally, this man, to his amazement, cried out: "Blessed are you Ibrahim, the Lord be with you." However, Ibrahim answered: "Do not get astonished, you are asking me for money which I am entrusted to, and an honest person should not be upset if someone asks him for a donation."

He also used to hold banquets for the poor at churches, and once he was at St. Barbara Church in Old Cairo and noticed that there was a bit of reluctance in serving the poor, so he rebuked those who were supposed to serve the poor saying: "Do not break the hearts of those simple poor people, but rather cheer them up, for Lord Christ ordered us to host those who can't pay us back."

Ibrahim was even charitable after his departure! A poor man came looking for him at his house but people told him that he passed away, and showed him his tomb. The man sat and kept crying and weeping till he fell asleep. In a vision he saw Contour Ibrahim saying: "Do not weep, a person named ...... owes me some money, go and take it." The poor man saw the vision three times, so he headed to that man and told him the story and found that it was true, and they both glorified the Lord.

After his departure, some wicked people told the governor that Demiana, Ibrahim's daughter, is keeping her father's money while the economical state of the country was deteriorating at that time. The governor called her and asked about the truth of the issue. Demiana didn't object but asked him for a few days to go and get the money and all her father's possessions. When she came back, she brought with her a huge number of the poor and needy whom her father used to help, telling the governor, the money of my father is in those poor peoples' stomachs. He then let her go in peace and hailed her charitable father.

That was just a glimpse of Contour Ibrahim El Gohary's life. He departed in peace in 1795 or 1796. The late H.G. Bishop Yousab Bishop of Gerga lamented him deeply saying: "Let us gather today, O priests and servants of the Lord, put on sackcloth to lament for the departure of him, who was always serving the churches with offerings and oblations."

Anba Abraam Bishop of Fayoum:

The renowned saint of the 20th century, the good shepherd and miracle performer... He had so many virtues, but the most prominent was his charitable deeds. After his ordination as a deputy for El Menya diocese, the headquarters became a place of dwelling for strangers and an orphanage for poor and needy people. When he was the Abbot of El Meharraq Monastery, he continued this charitable practice, yet some monks didn't agree with it and accused him of wasting the monastery's money. He was subsequently deprived of his position and expelled totally from that monastery!

When he was ordained as a Bishop of Fayyoum in 1881, he kept performing the same virtue, to the extent of giving all he owned...

Once a poor person went asking for help as his wife had

just given birth to a baby and he had no money to support the child. Anba Abraam gave him one Egyptian pound. On his way back, the deputy saw a pound with that man, so he took it and gave him 20 Piasters instead, so the poor man came back and informed Anba Abraam, who called the deputy and rebuked him for his hard-heartedness and lack of faith, and ordered him to give the one pound back to the poor man, as well as a quilt for the present winter. The deputy objected claiming that the diocese was in real need for that money, but the man of God answered, God will send. A few minutes after the poor man left, one of the believers sent the sum of ten Egyptian Pounds and many wheat sacks for the monastery.

On a different occasion, a poor lady came asking for money, but he didn't have any at that time. So he gave her his shawl as a present. He told her to go and sell the shawl and use the money. When she went to the market, the man who gave the shawl as a present to Anba Abraam saw it, so he bought it from the woman and headed to Anba Abraam, but before showing him the shawl he asked him, "My father, why aren't you wearing the shawl, it is winter now and freezing cold?" The Bishop answered, "The shawl is up my son" i.e. with Jesus, then the man gave him the shawl back, but Anba Abraam asked, "Maybe you were unjust to her my son?" But the man answered, "No my father, I gave her its full price."

We still hear a lot about this blessed saint who gave us a great example of asceticism, poverty and love for the poor and needy. May the Lord grant us to follow in his footsteps, and accept our prayers through his great intercession.

www.ingramcontent.com/pod-product-compliance
Lightning Source LLC
Chambersburg PA
CBHW022126080426
42734CB00006B/244